I0559544

VEHICLES

Dot Marker Coloring Book Sheets for Kids Ages 1–5

Interactive Pages with Games for Kids Under 5 | Fun Scissor Practice, Maze Puzzles, Counting Activities and Pre K Weekly Spelling for Toddlers & Preschoolers

POLYMATH Panda

ISBN: 978-1-953149-76-3

This Book Belongs To:

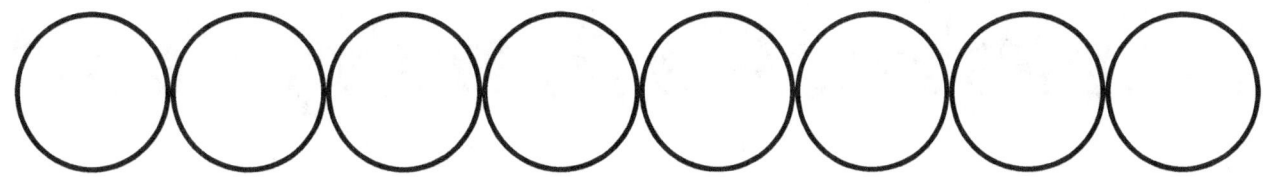

Grab Your Dot Markers and Dive into 50 Fun-Filled Pages of Cars, Trucks, Trains, and many more!

Featuring a wide variety of vehicles including cars, jeeps, trains, helicopters, airplanes, fire trucks, ambulances, and more. Includes engaging activities like I Spy, Counting, Mazes, Color Matching, and Size Recognition, all designed with large, easy-to-color dots. Perfectly compatible with all leading dot marker brands with consistent 0.75 inch (18mm) dots.

This book is a fantastic fit for young explorers aged 2 - 5. It's crafted to enhance your child's early learning journey with delightful vehicle designs that connect words, images, and colors. Our team of skilled designers has ensured each page stimulates your child's imagination and helps build their fine motor skills, making learning an exciting adventure!

We understand the enthusiasm of young dot marker artists, so we've designed each page to be single-sided, minimizing the risk of colors bleeding through. Additionally, placing a sheet of paper or card between the pages can be a great way to keep everything tidy!

Thank you for choosing this book! We hope it brings you and your child countless hours of dot marker joy and learning.

Free Printable Activity Book!

- **Enhances Creativity:** Fun dot marker coloring pages.
- **Builds Fine Motor Skills:** Scissor skill exercises and dot-to-dot puzzles.
- **Boosts Cognitive Development:** Simple addition with numbers and images.
- **Encourages Observation:** Engaging I Spy games.
- **Hours of Fun:** Full kawaii coloring pages designed for young children.

QR Code in the Back of the Book

Enjoying this Book?

We'd love to hear your thoughts

We may just send
you something special.

Rocket

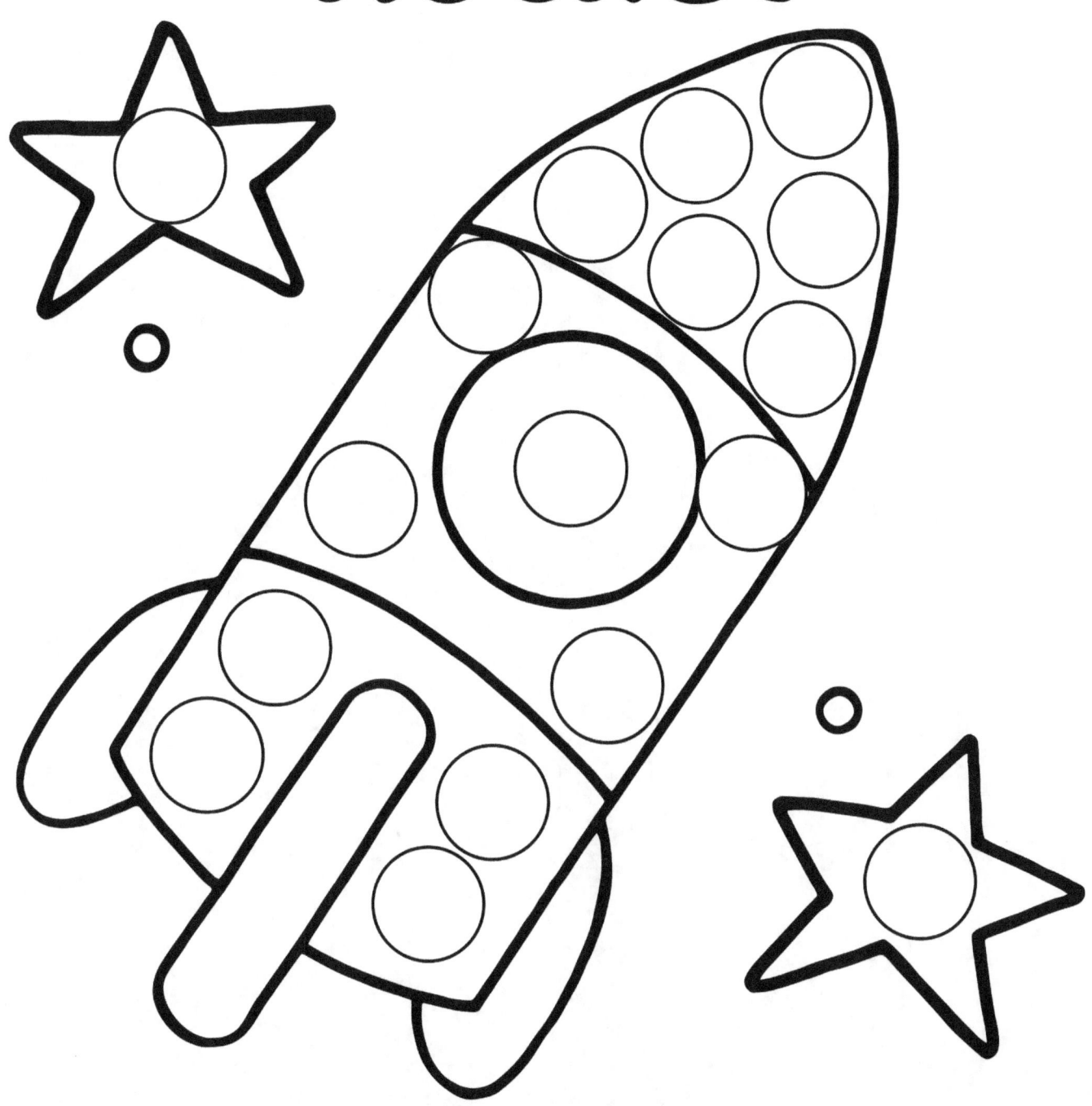

Spell out "Rocket" by dotting each letter

R　　o　　c　　k　　e　　t

Week 1

Scissor Practice

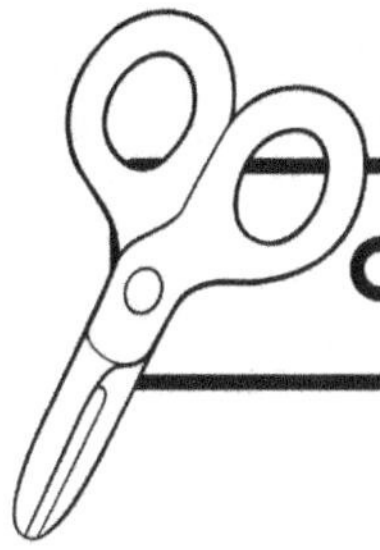

Cut along the dotted line to practice your scissor skills.

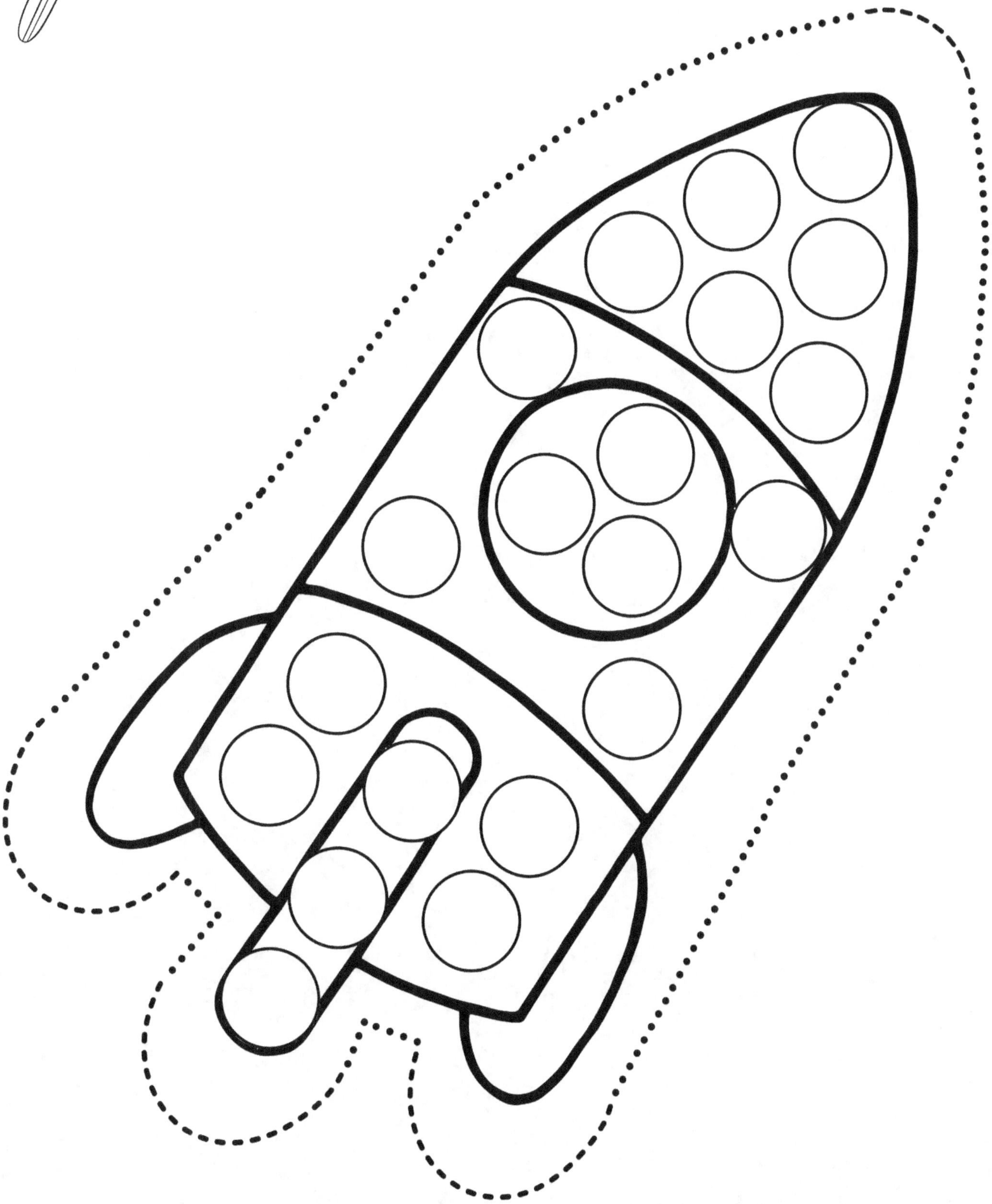

Week 1

I Spy

 **Find the Rocket and dot it.**

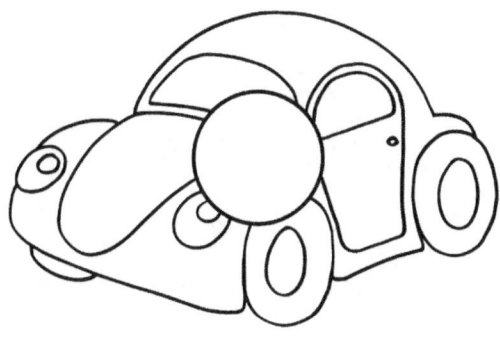

Maze

Dot the circles to help
Ethan find the rocket.

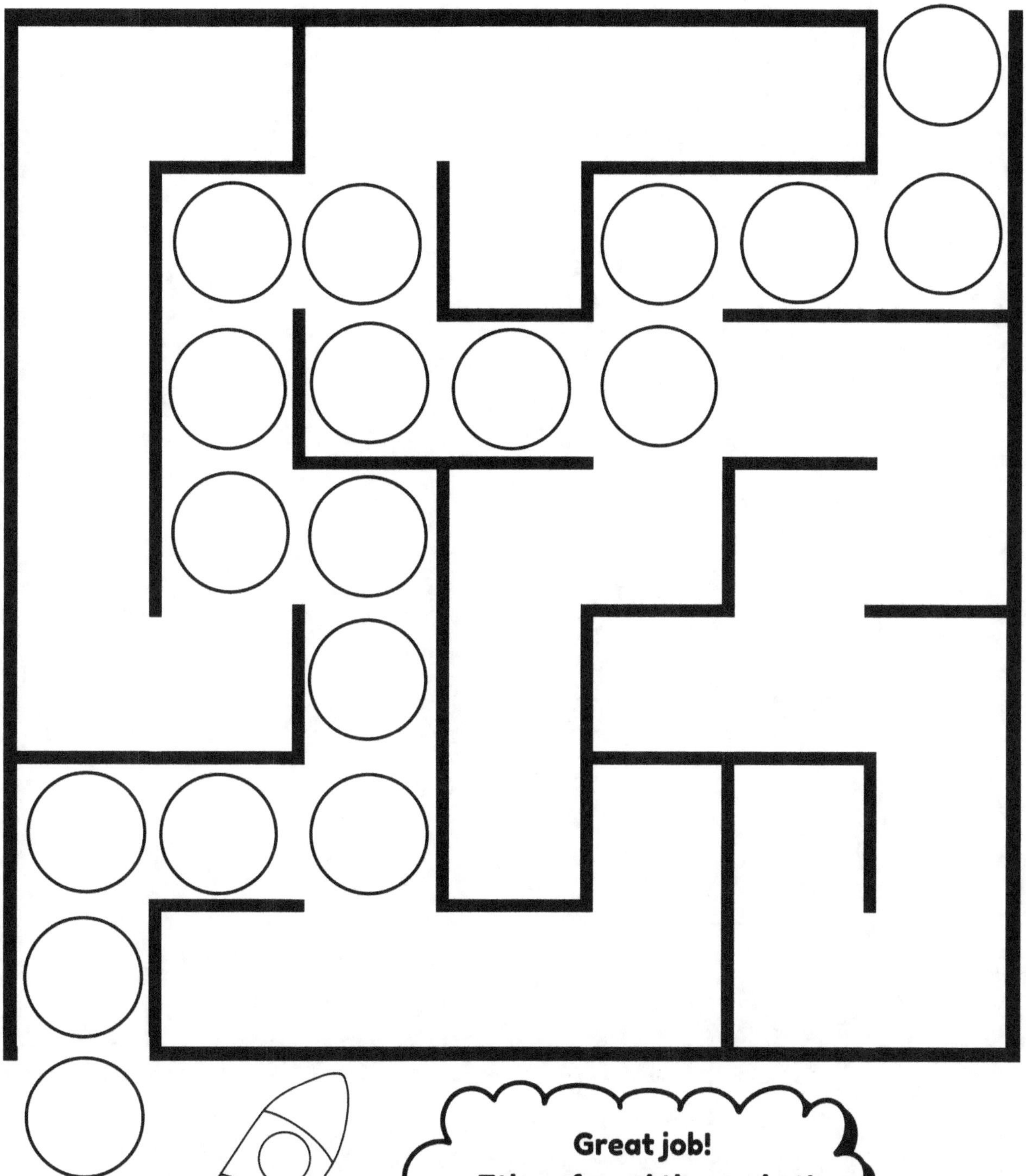

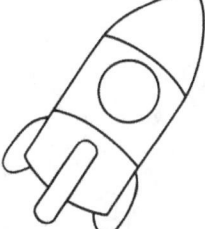

Great job!
Ethan found the rocket!

Week 2

Beetle

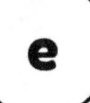

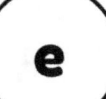

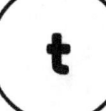

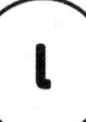

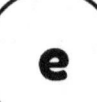

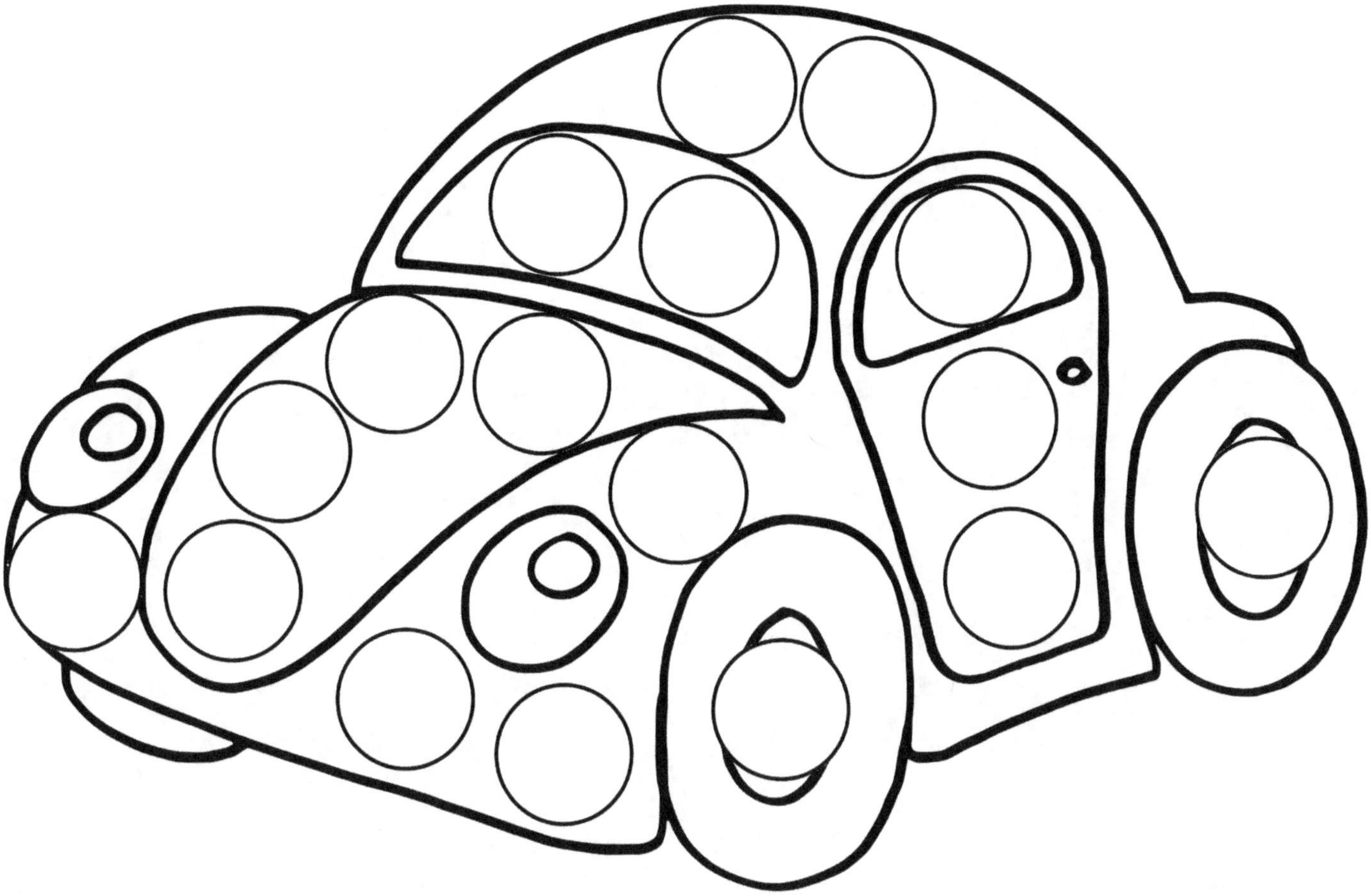

Spell out "Beetle" by dotting each letter

B e e t l e

Week 2

Scissor Practice

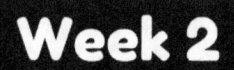

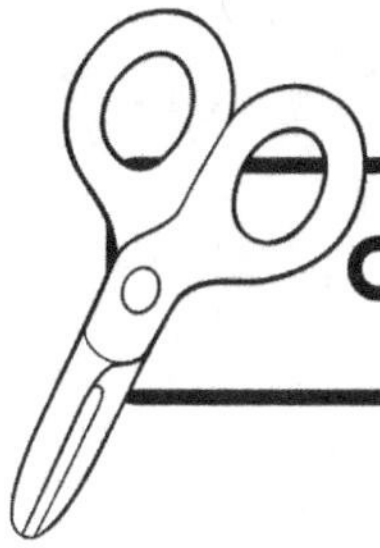

Cut along the dotted line to practice your scissor skills.

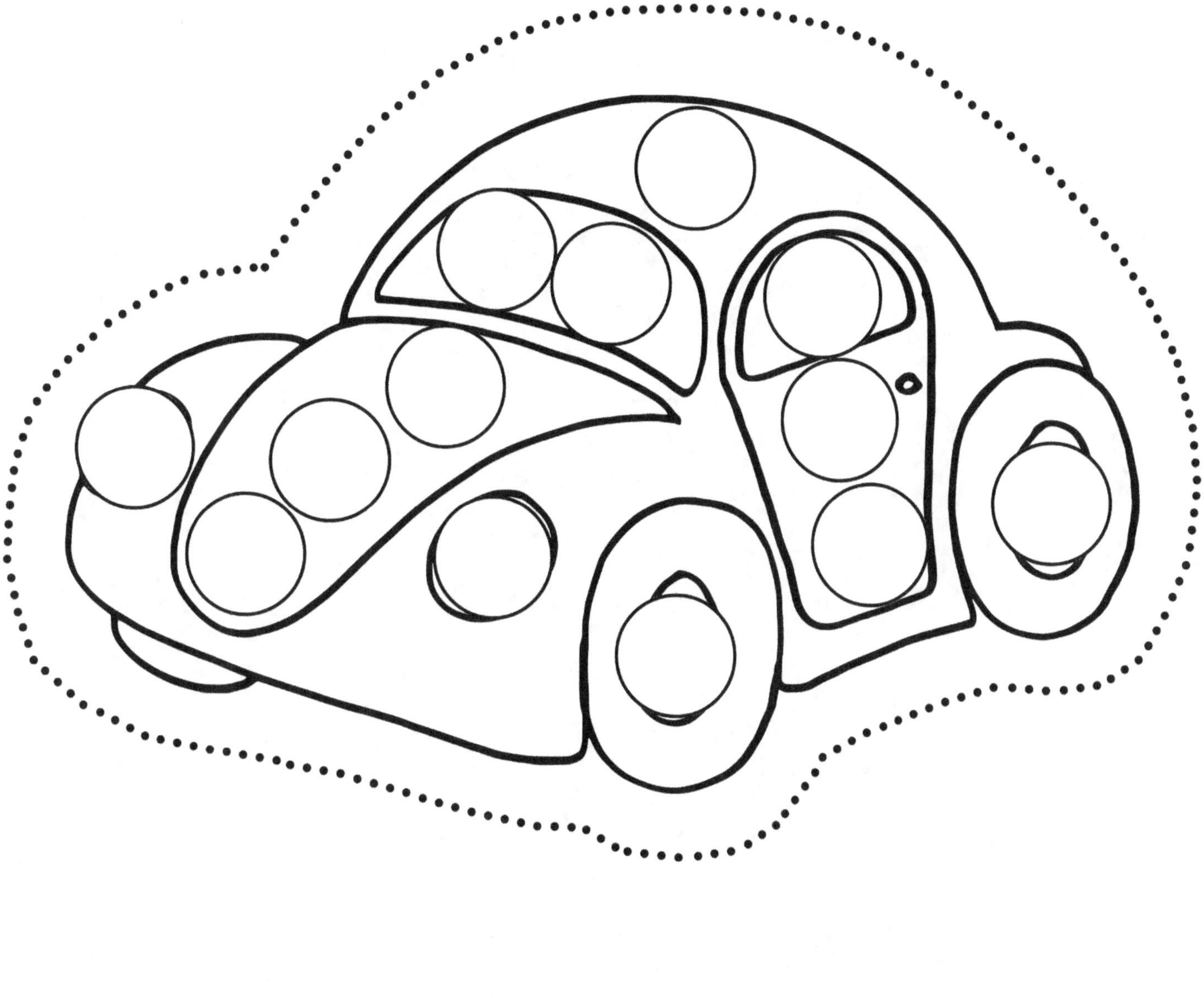

Color Match

 **Dot all Beetles Red**

 **Dot all Rockets Blue**

 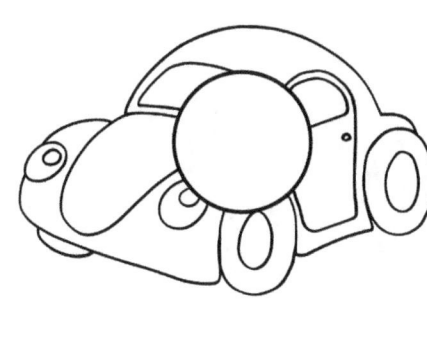 

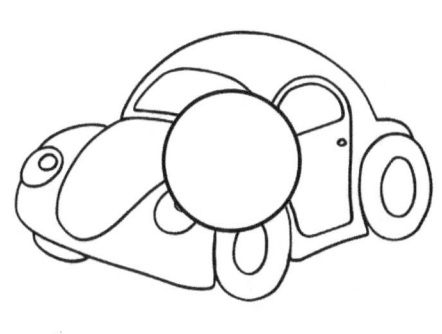  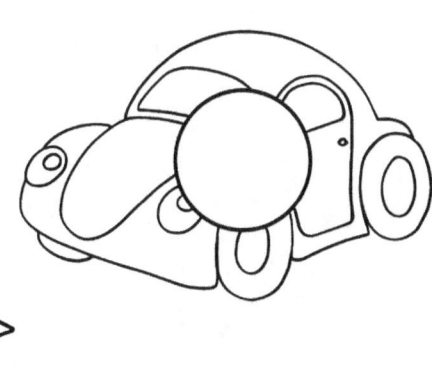

 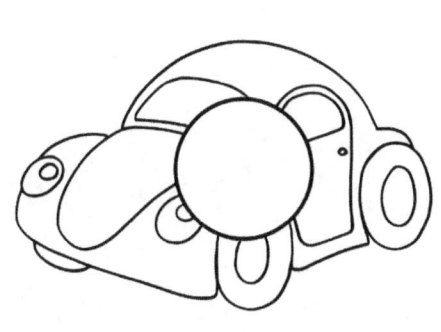 

Dot 2 Submarines

Dot 1 Beetle

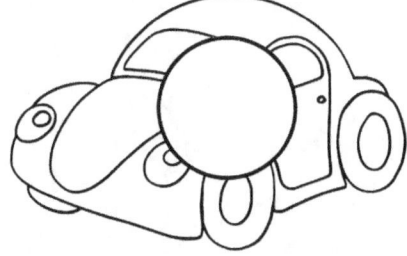
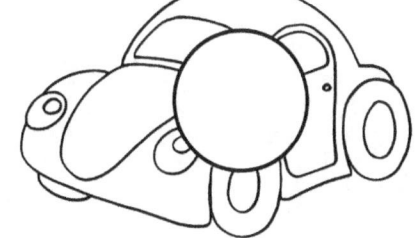
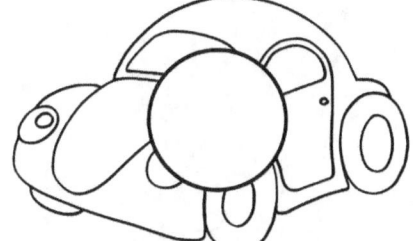
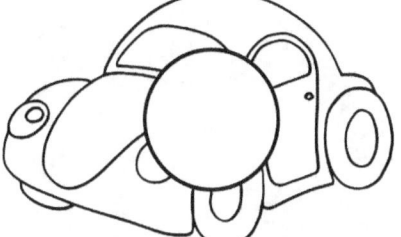

Scooter

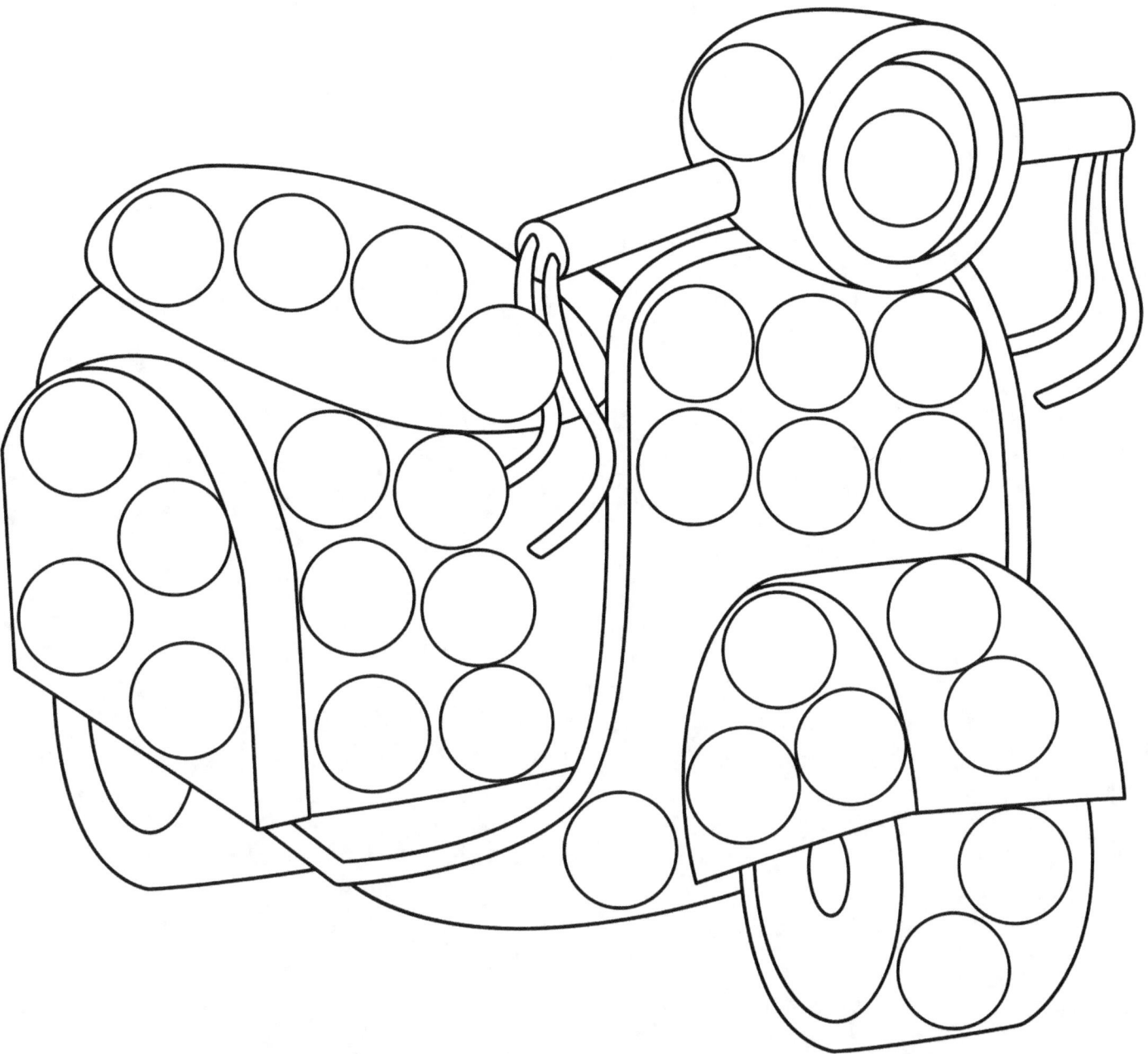

Spell out "Scooter" by dotting each letter

S c o o t e r

Week 3

Scissor Practice

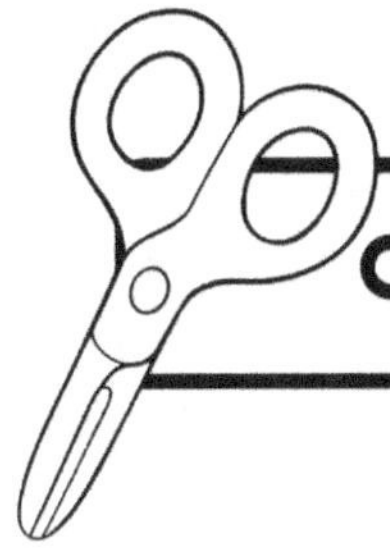

Cut along the dotted line to practice your scissor skills.

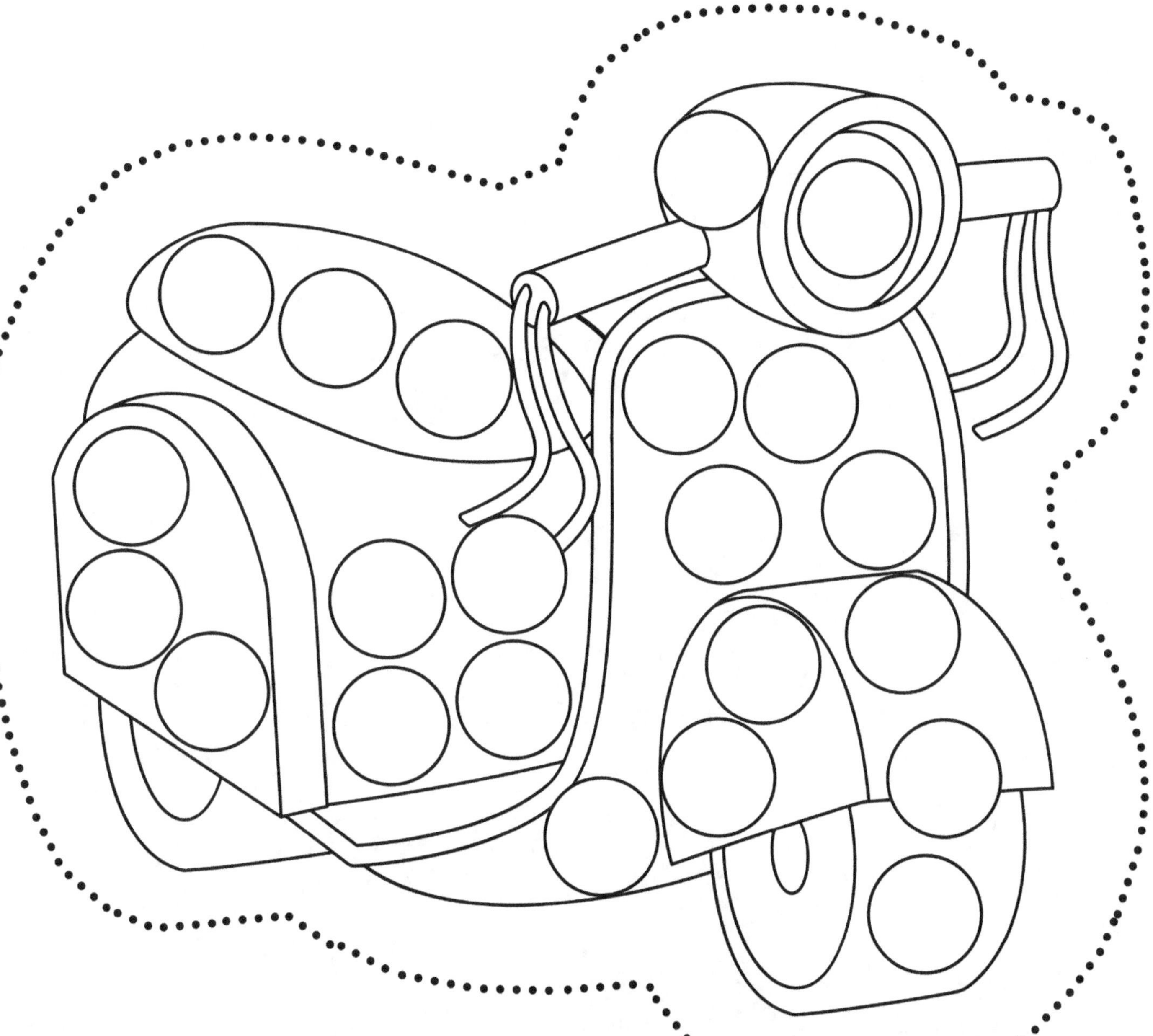

Color Match

Dot all Scooters Green

Dot all Rockets Violet

 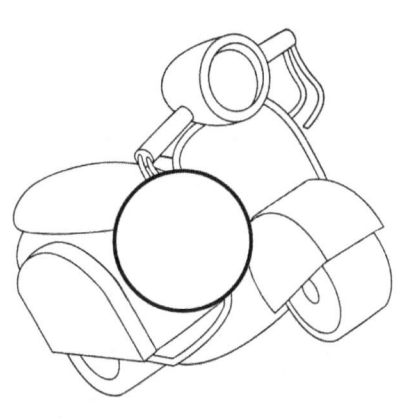 

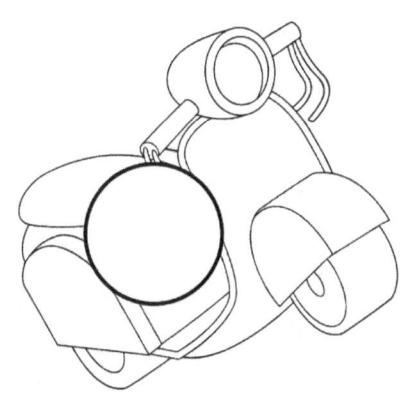  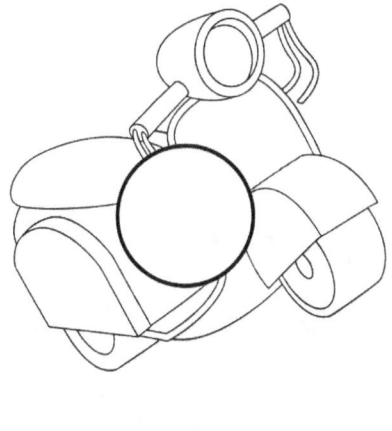

 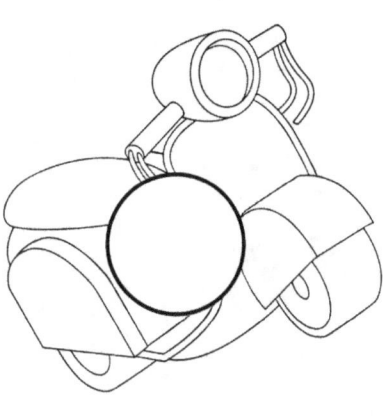 

Week 3

Maze

Dot the circles to help Luke find his scooter!

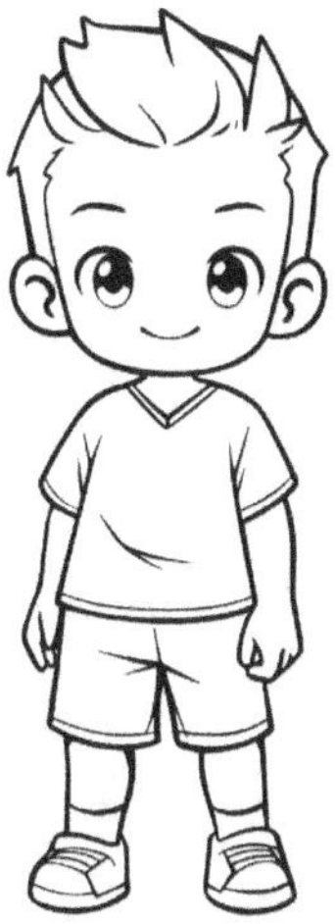

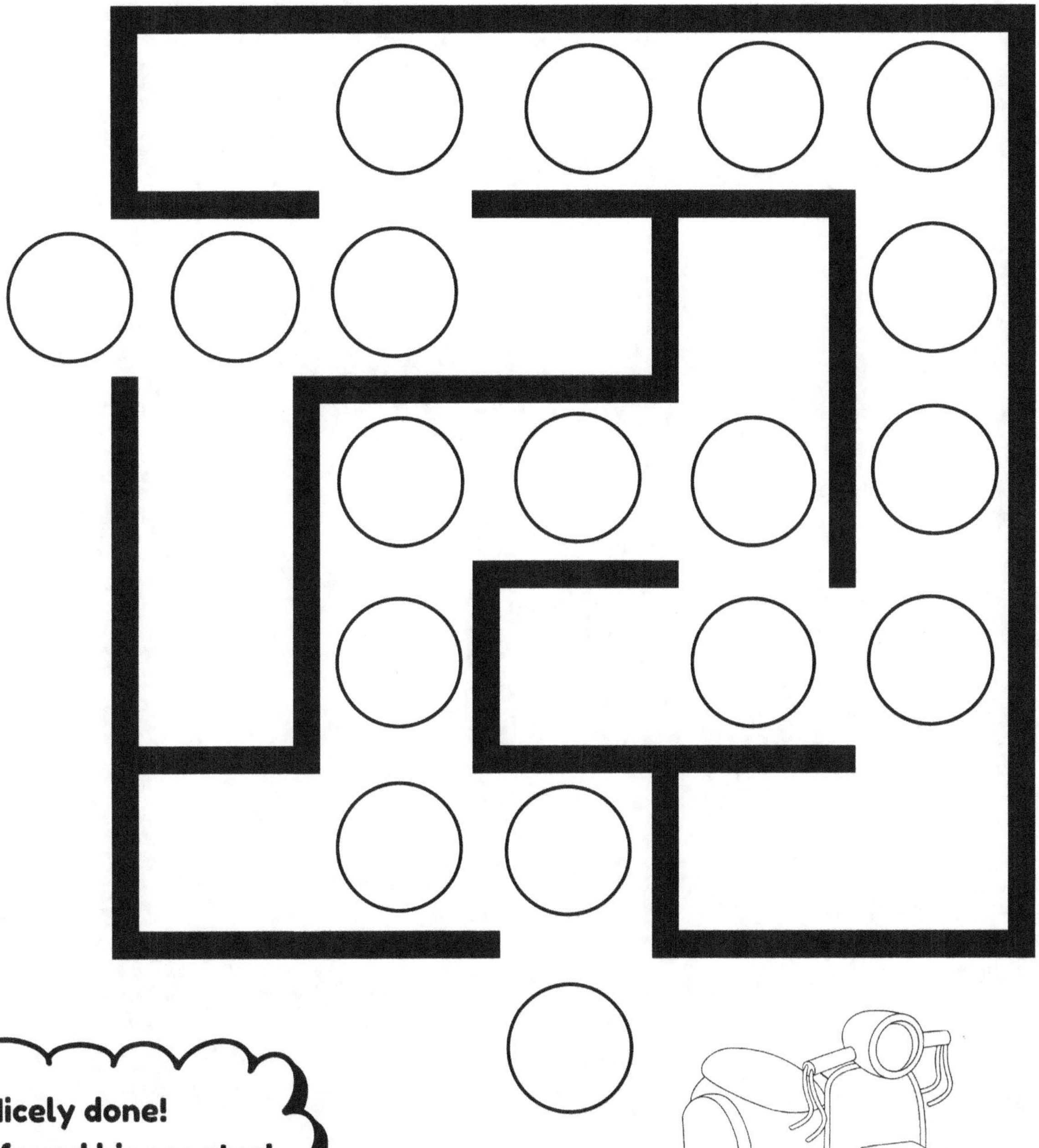

"Nicely done! Michael found his scooter!

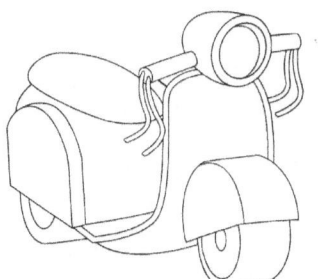

Submarine

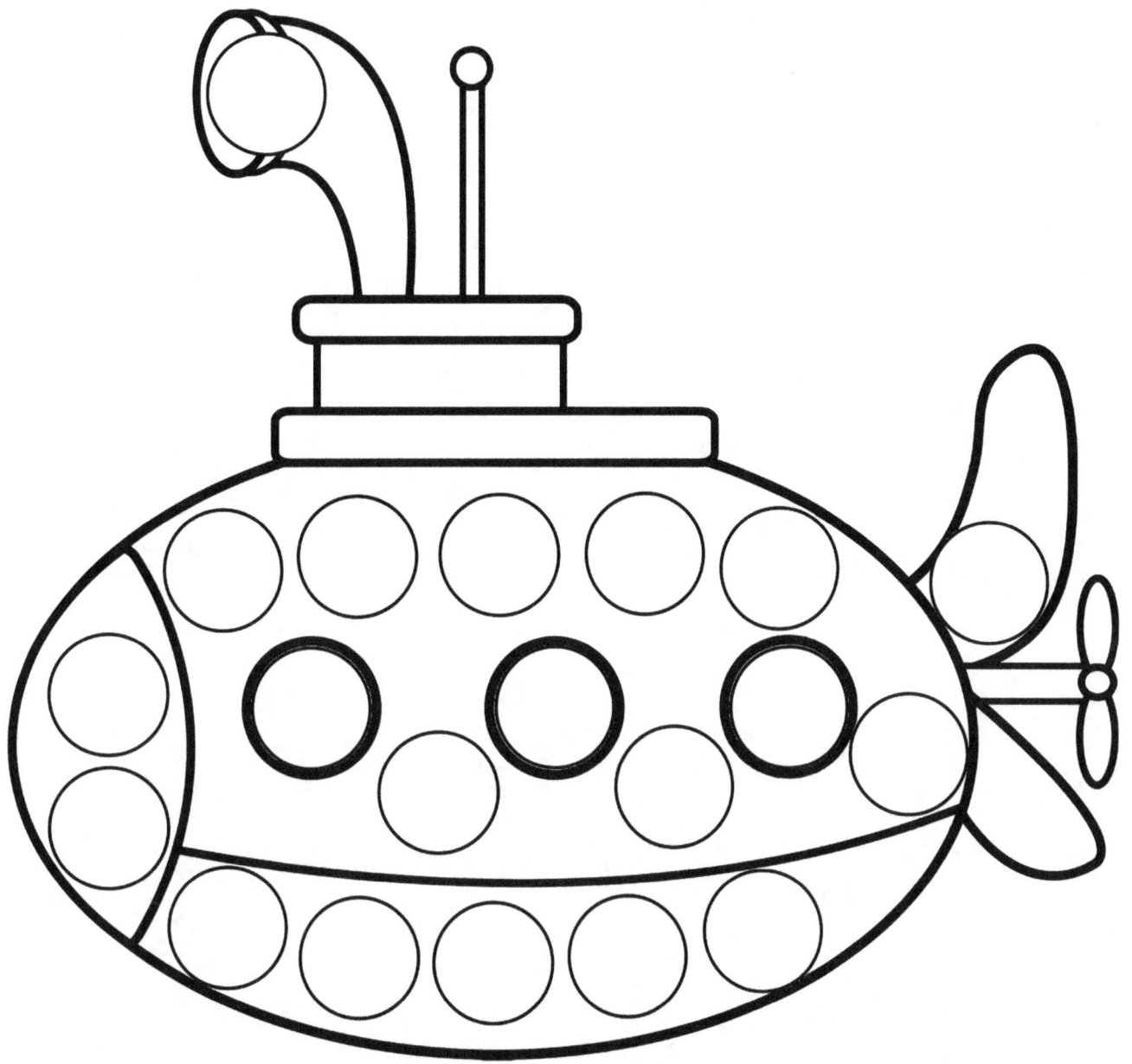

Spell out "Submarine" by dotting each letter

S   u   b   m   a   r   i   n   e

Week 4

Scissor Practice

Cut along the dotted line to practice your scissor skills.

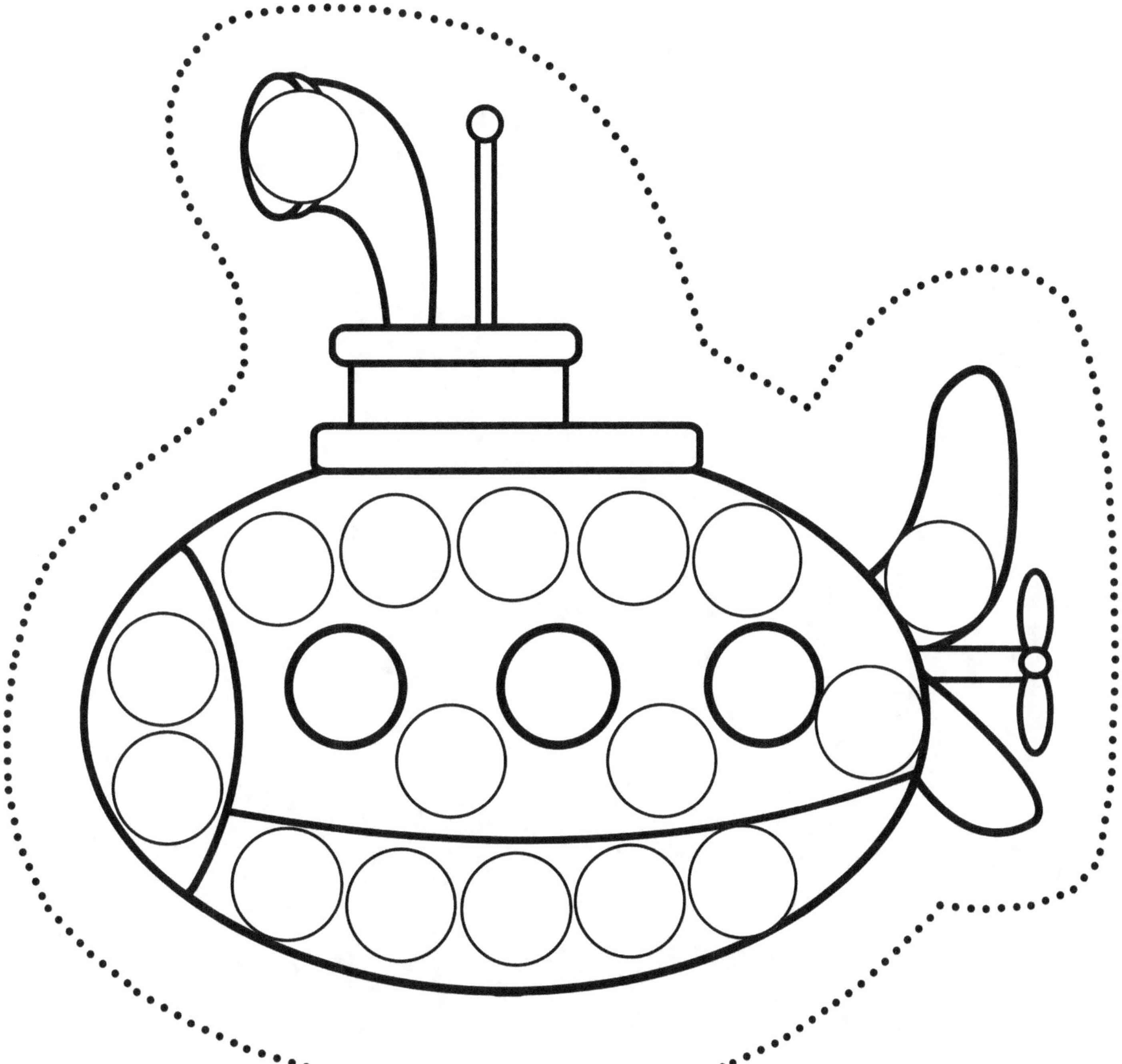

Dot all Submarines Violet ······ **Dot all Scooters Orange**

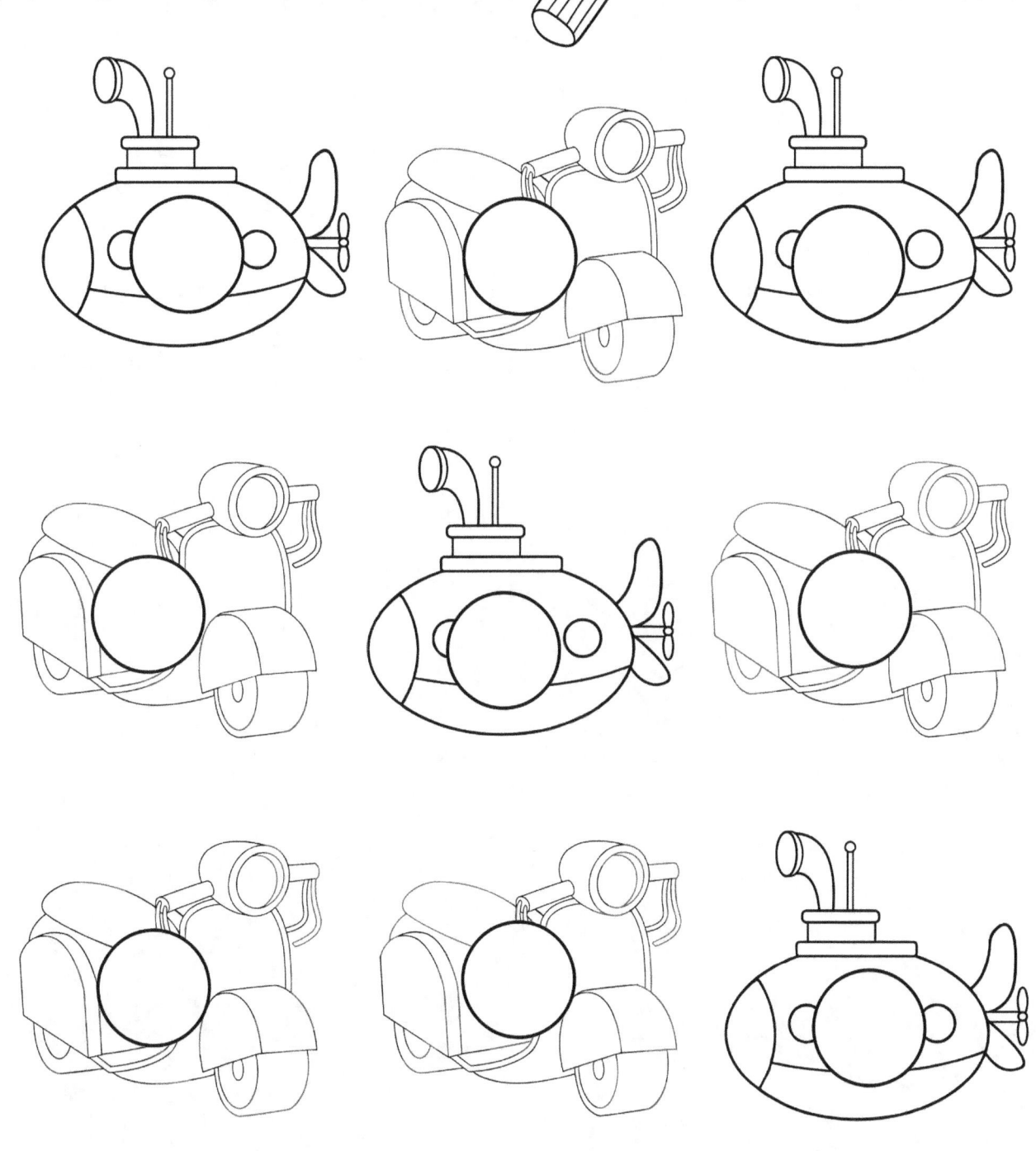

Dot 3 Submarines

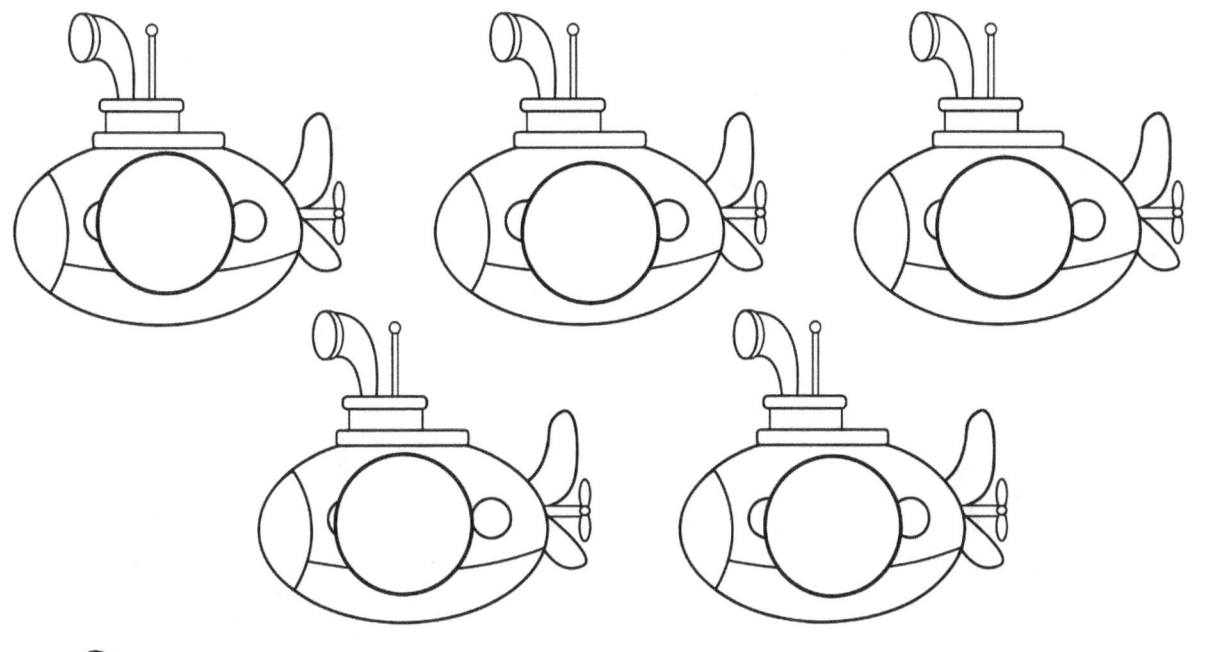

Dot 1 Taxi

Airplane

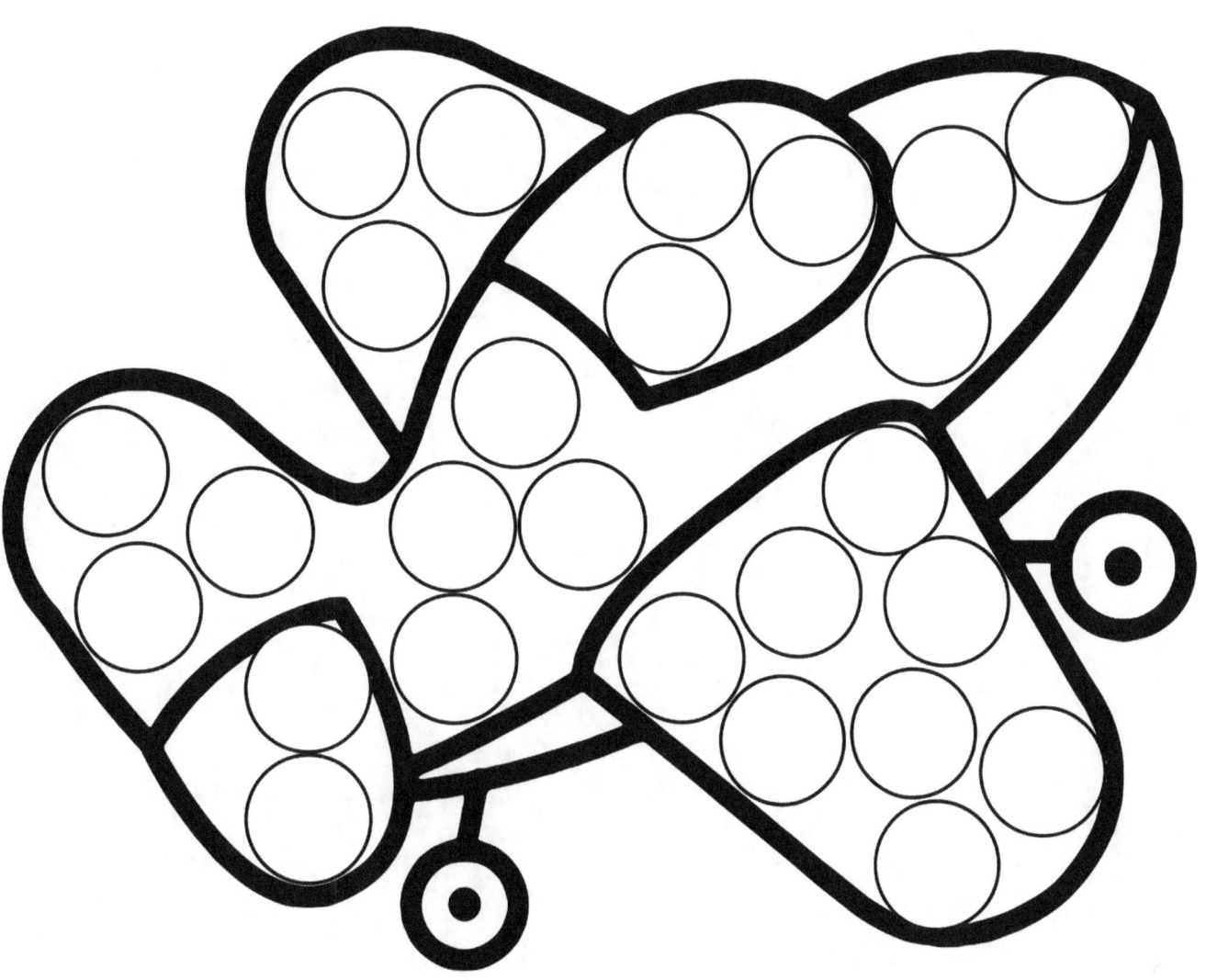

Spell out "Airplane" by dotting each letter

(A) (i) (r) (p) (l) (a) (n) (e)

Week 5

Scissor Practice

Cut along the dotted line to practice your scissor skills.

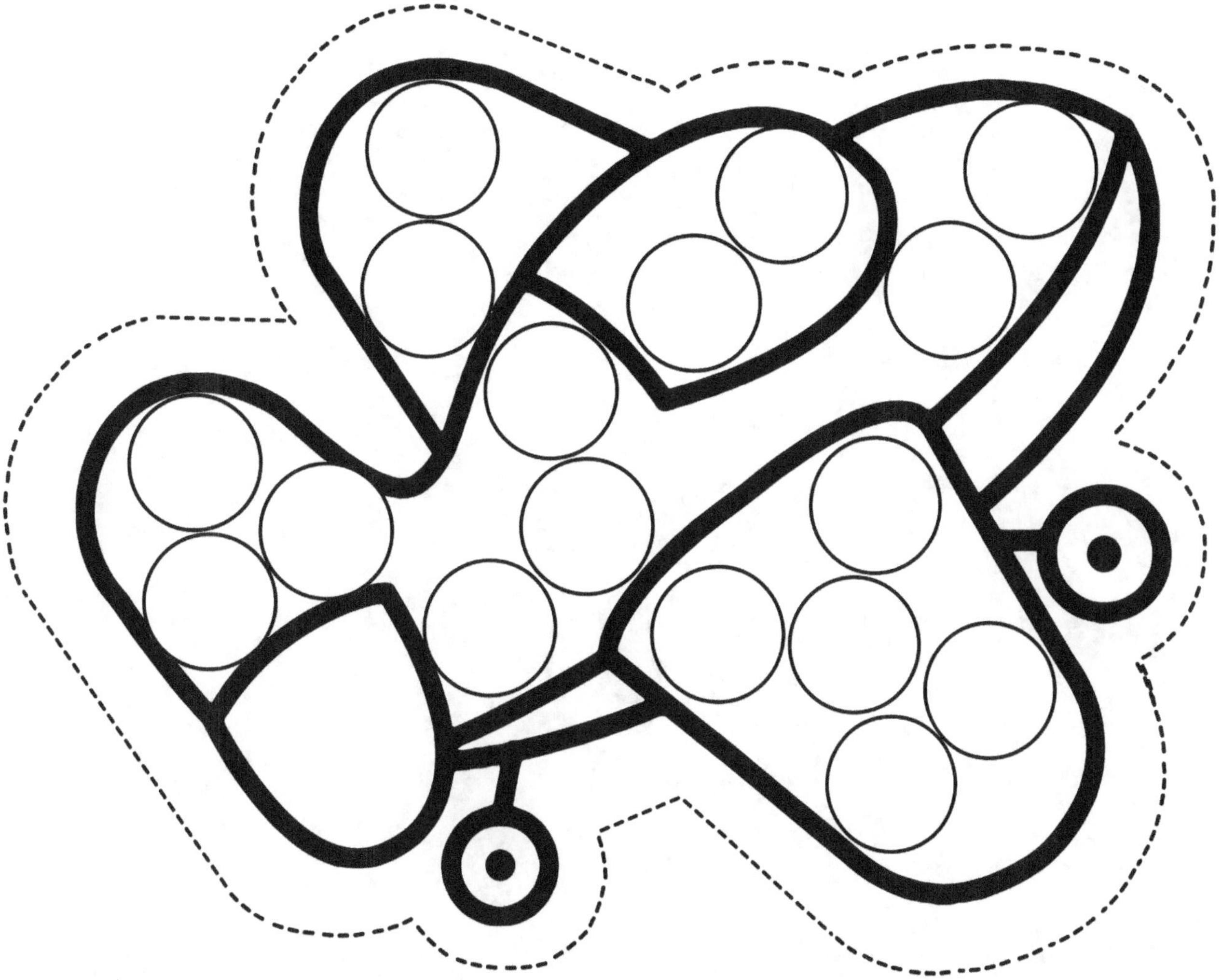

I SPY Find the Airplane and dot it.

Maze

Dot the circles to help the pilot find the airplane!

"Nicely done!
The pilot found the airplane!

Airship

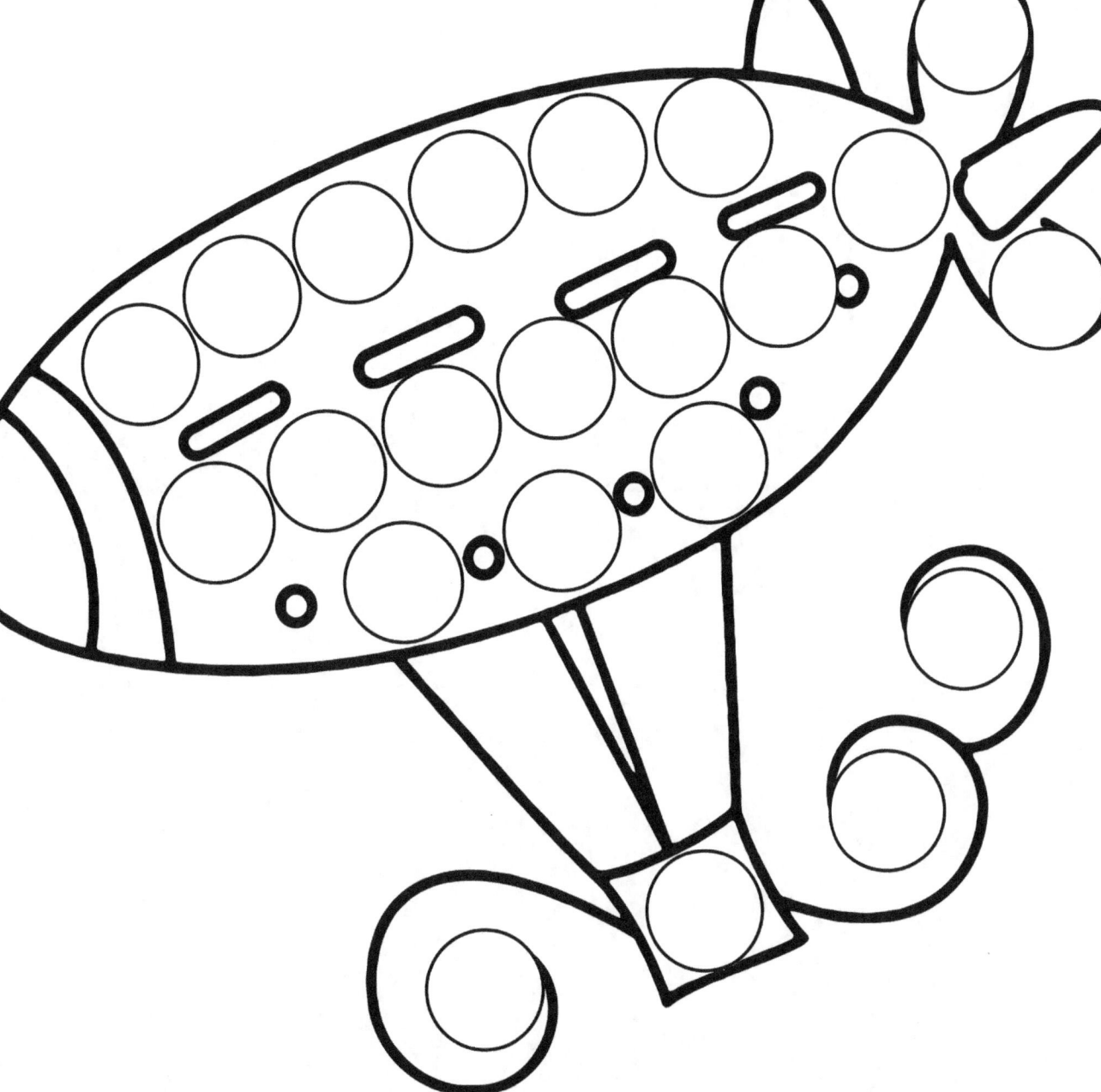

Spell out "Airship" by dotting each letter

(A) (i) (r) (s) (h) (i) (p)

Week 6

Scissor Practice

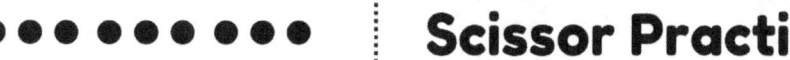

Cut along the dotted line to practice your scissor skills.

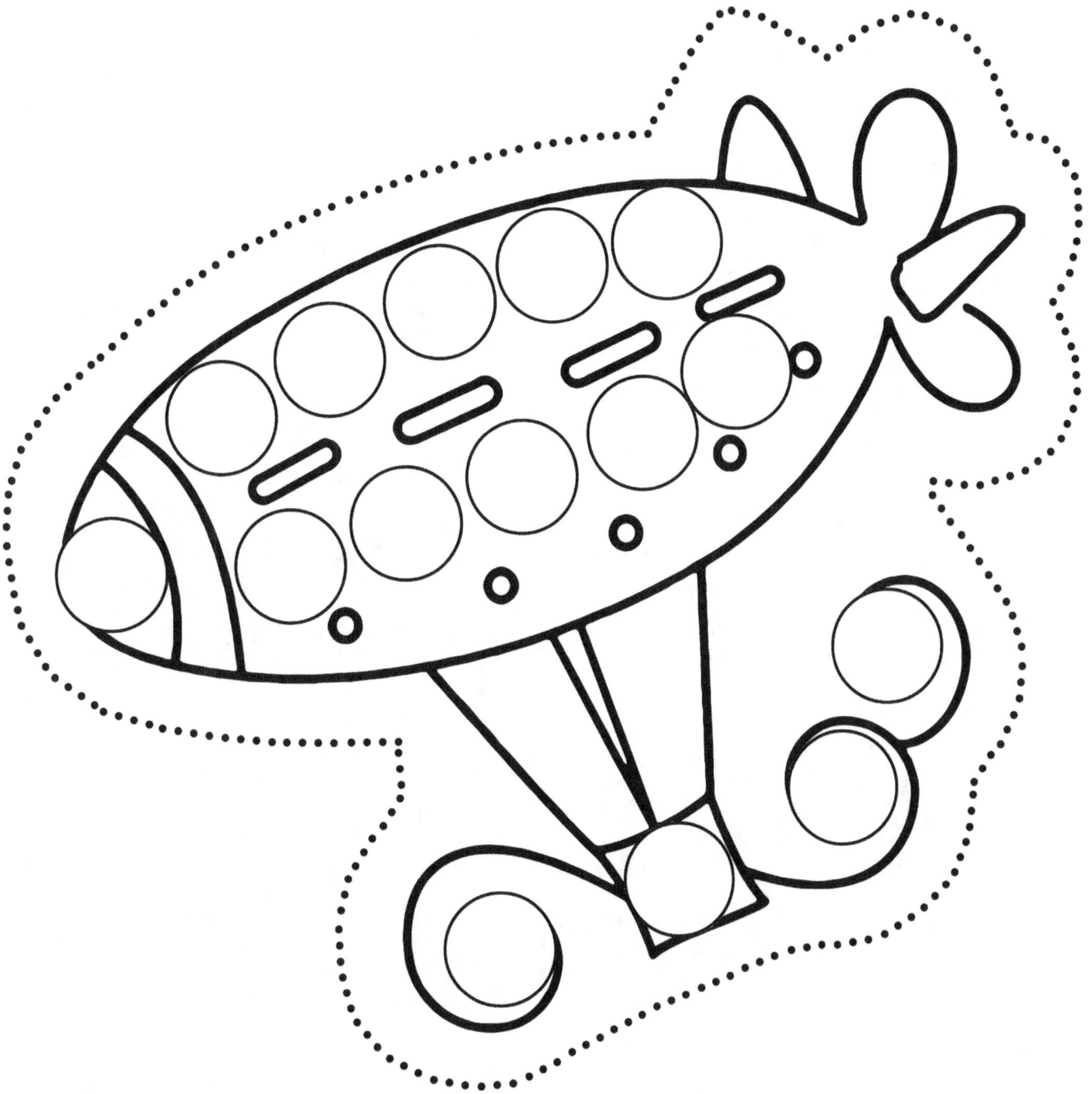

Week 6

Color Match

 **Dot all Airships Orange**

 **Dot all Helicopters Blue**

Dot 1 Airship

Dot 3 Helicopters

Ambulance

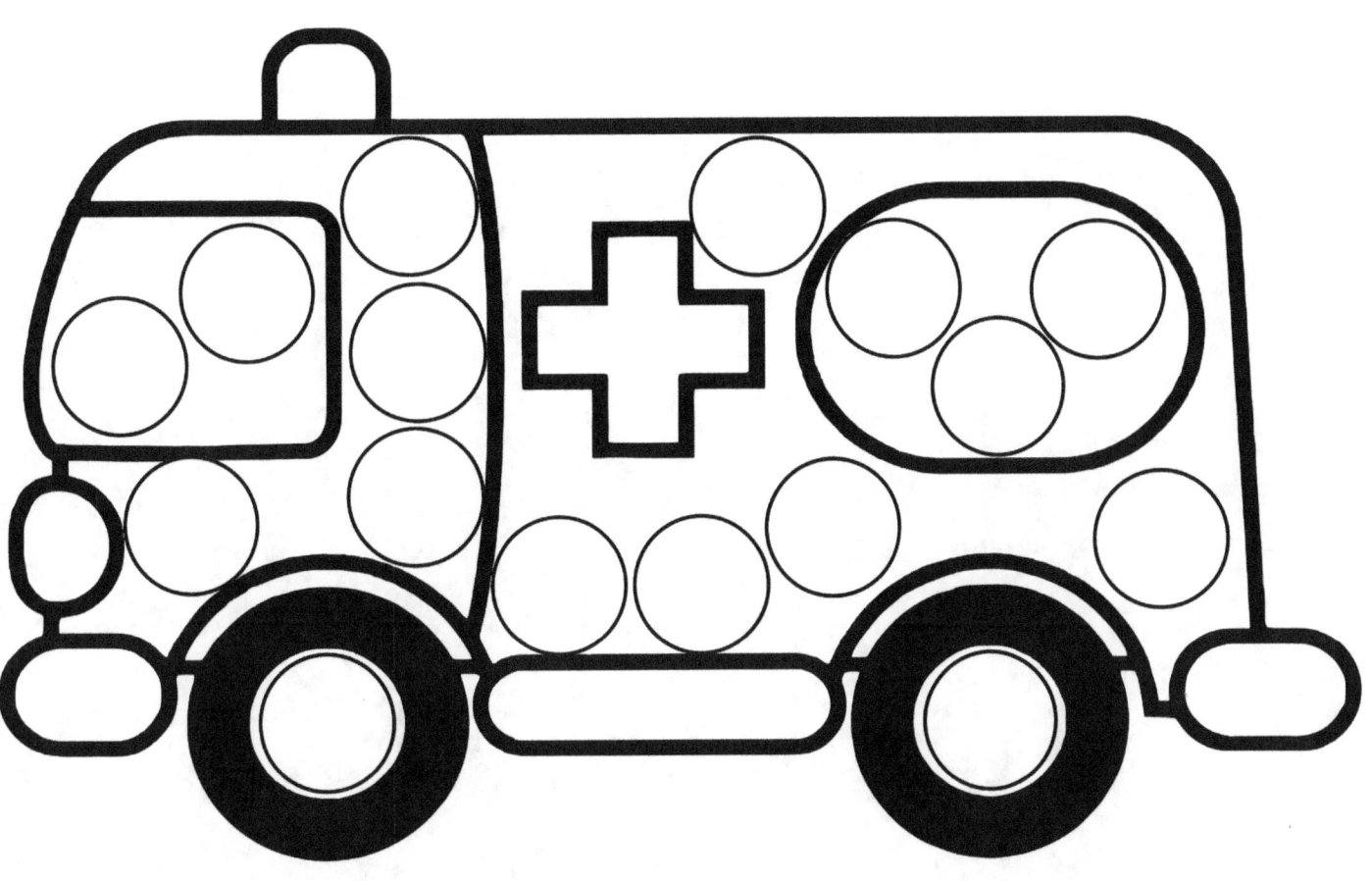

Spell out "Ambulance" by dotting each letter

(A) (m) (b) (u) (l) (a) (n) (c) (e)

Cut along the dotted line to practice your scissor skills.

I Spy

I SPY Find the Ambulance and dot it.

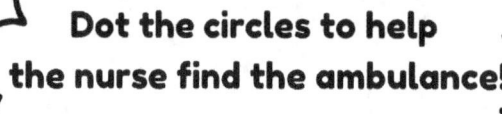

Dot the circles to help the nurse find the ambulance!

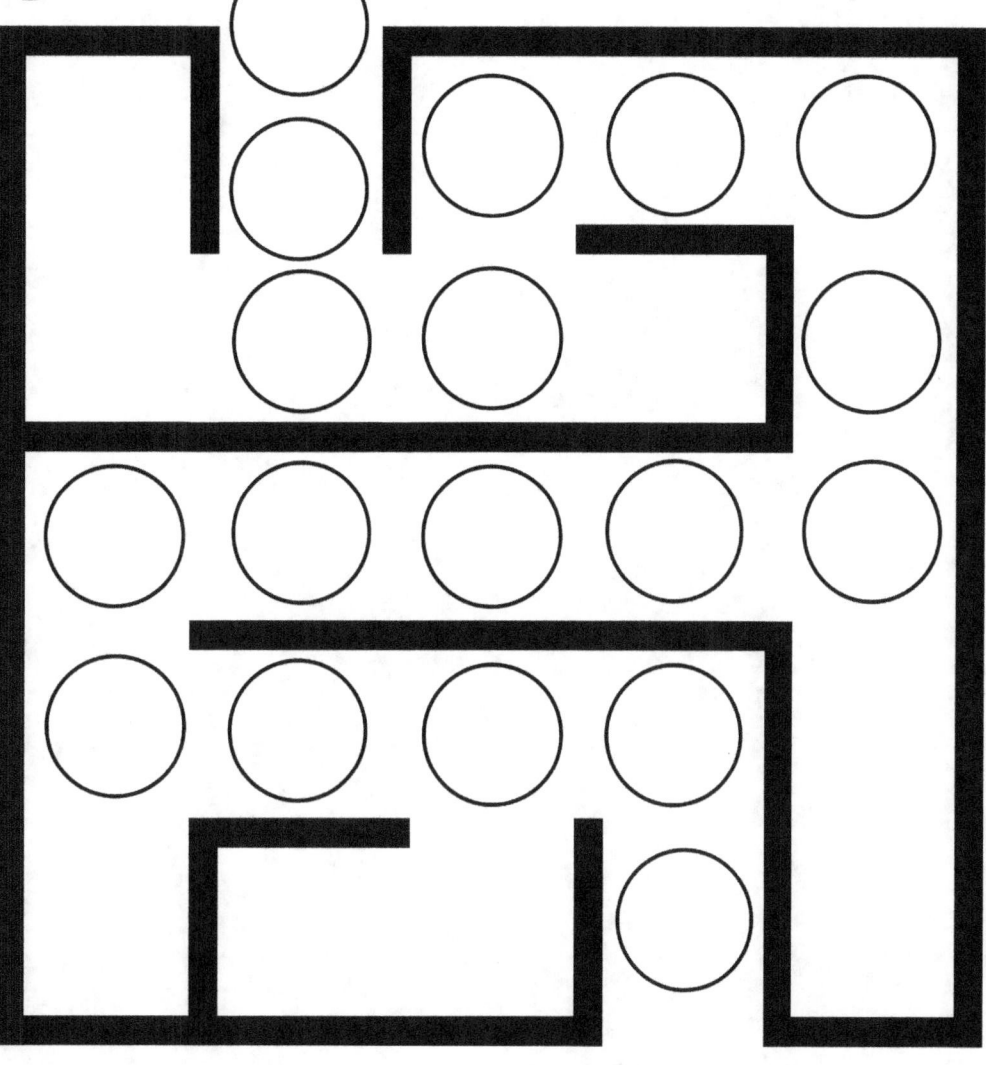

Good Job!
The nurse found the ambulance!

Week 8

Helicopter

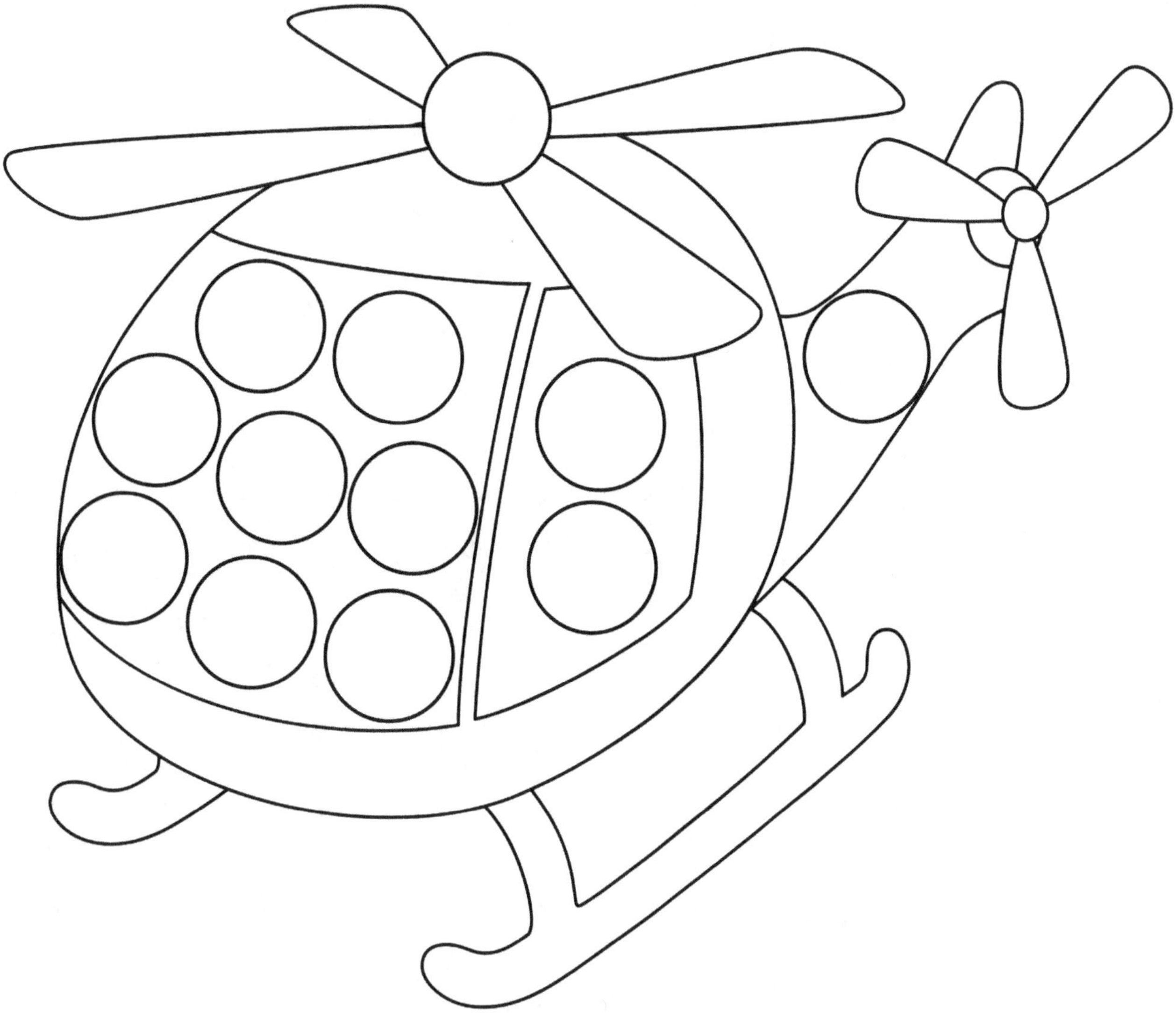

Spell out "Helicopter" by dotting each letter

H e l i c -

o p t e r

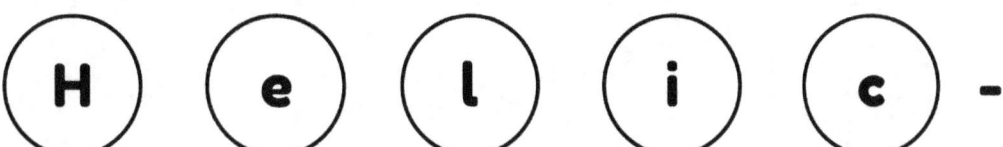

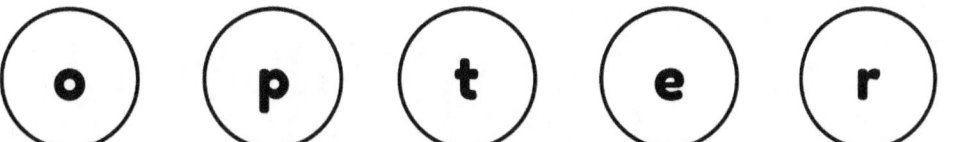

Scissor Practice

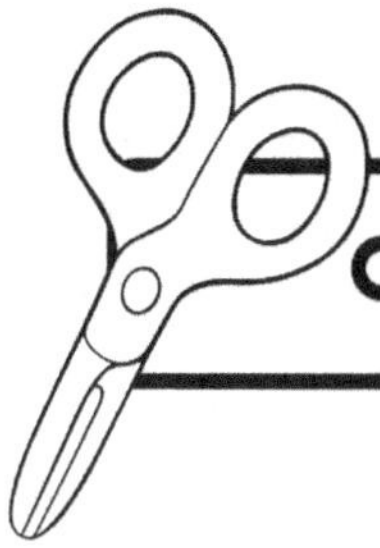

Cut along the dotted line to practice your scissor skills.

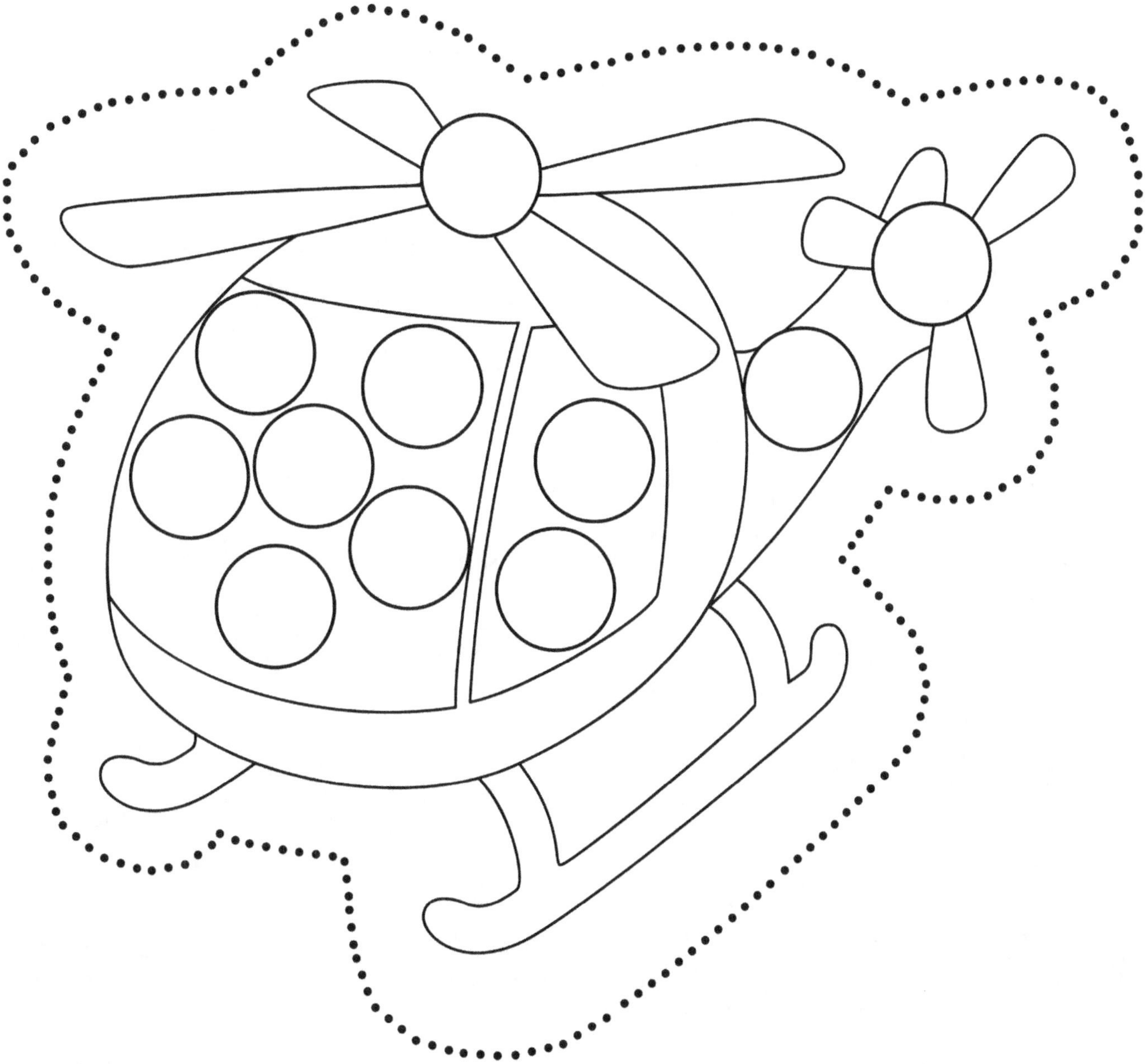

Color Match

Dot all Helicopters Blue

Dot all Ambulances Red

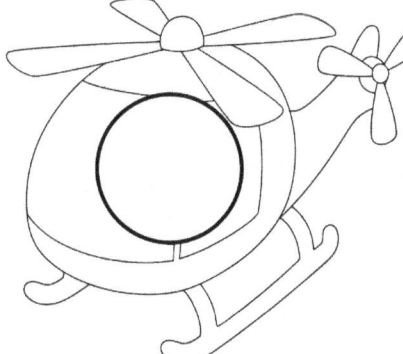

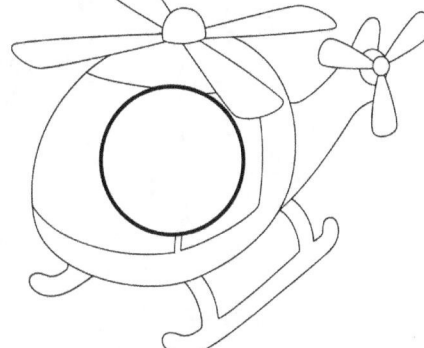
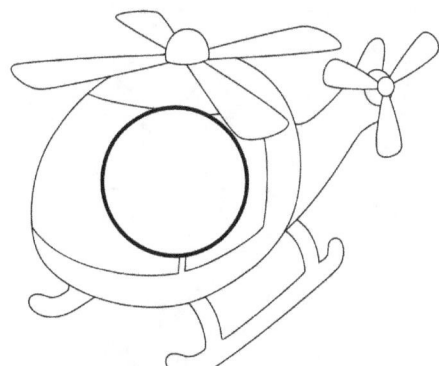

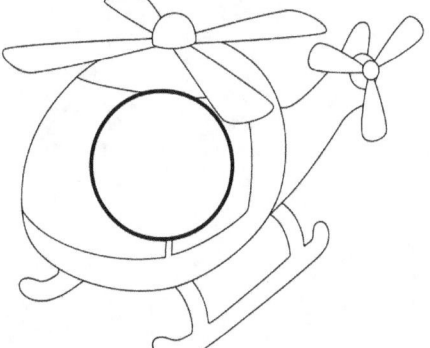

Counting

Dot 1 Helicopters.

Dot 4 Trains.

Tractor

Spell out "Tractor" by dotting each letter

T   r   a   c   t   o   r

Week 9

Scissor Practice

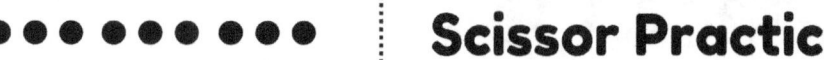

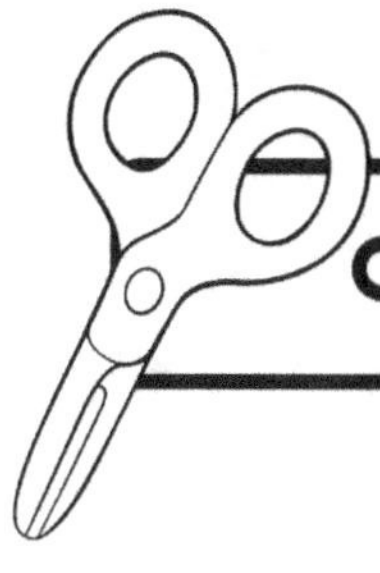

Cut along the dotted line to practice your scissor skills.

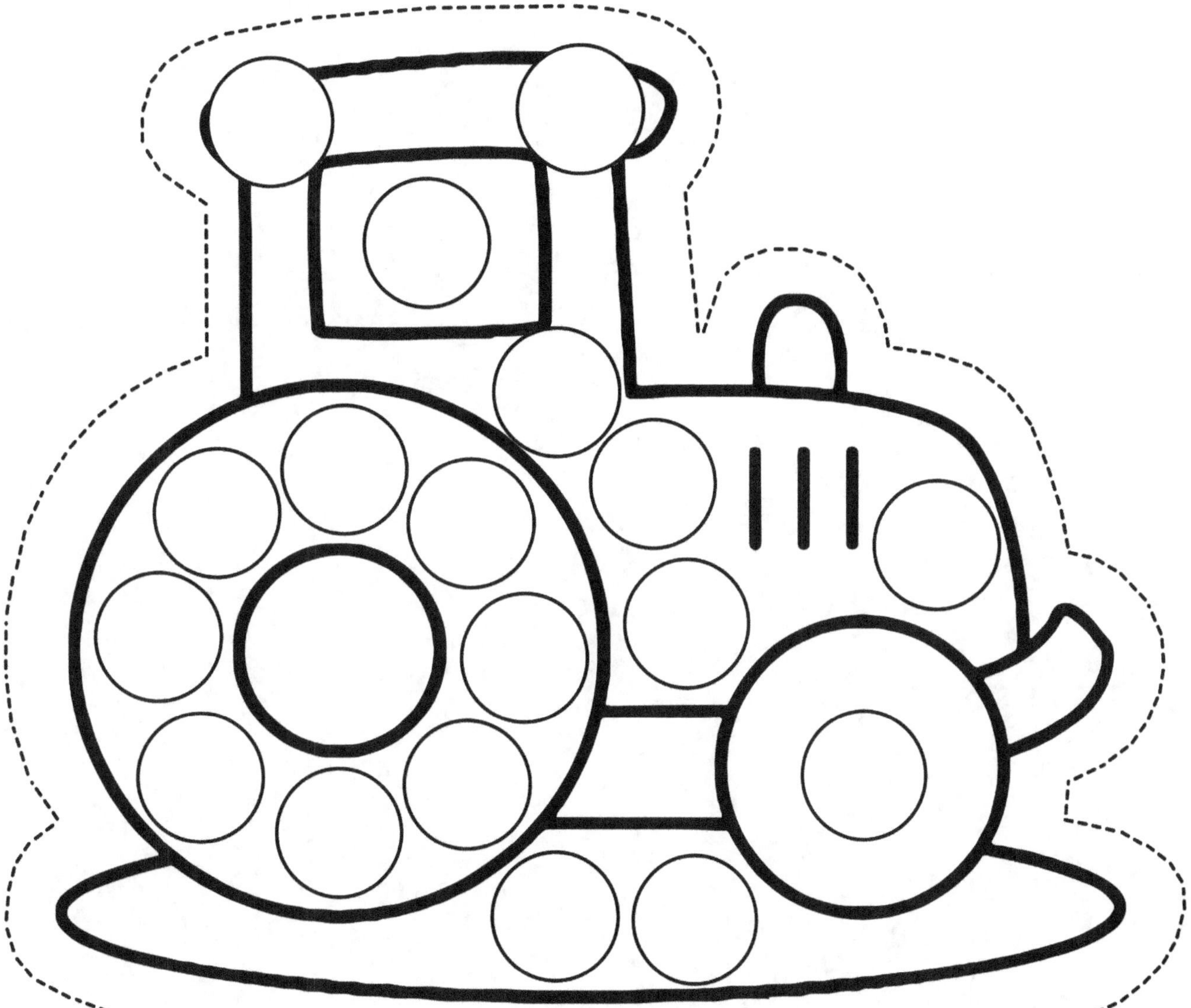

Week 9

I Spy

I SPY **Find the Tractor and dot it.**

35

Maze

Dot the circles to help the farmer find his tractor!

Well done!
The farmer found the tractor!

Week 10

Ship

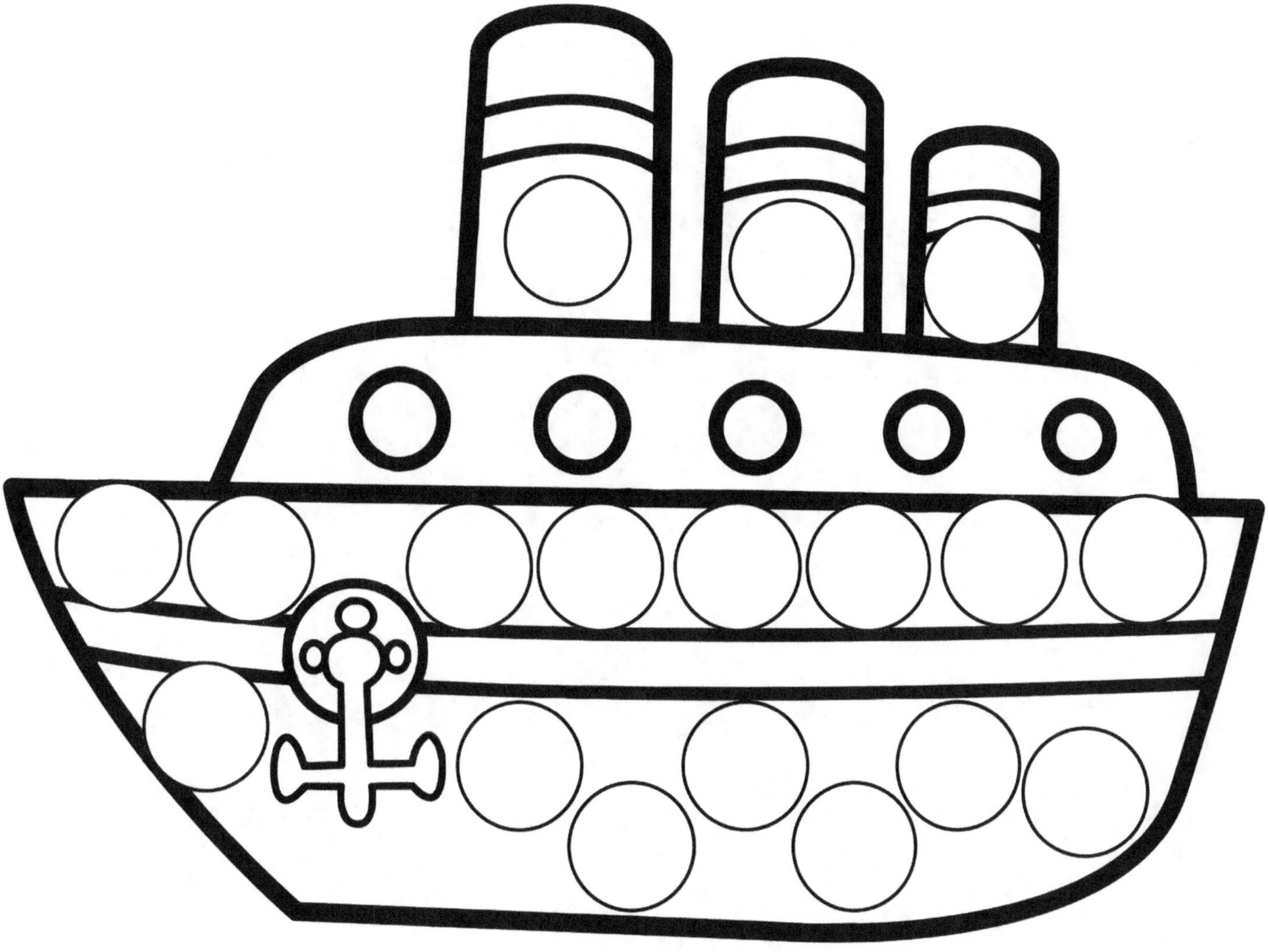

Spell out "Ship" by dotting each letter

S h i p

Scissor Practice

Cut along the dotted line to practice your scissor skills.

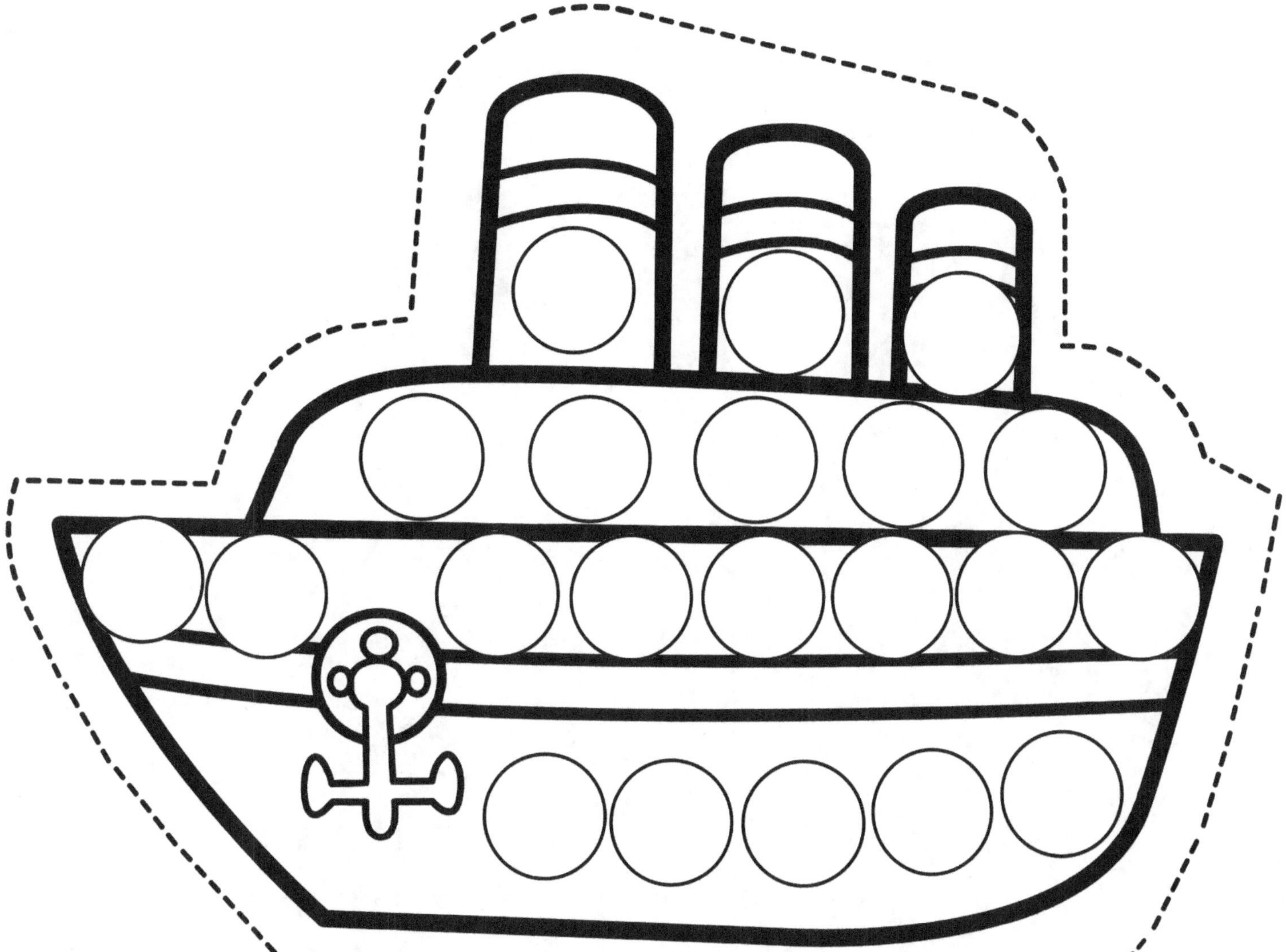

Color Match

Dot all Ships Yellow  **Dot all Tractors Orange**

Dot 2 Ships

Dot 5 Tractors

Sailboat

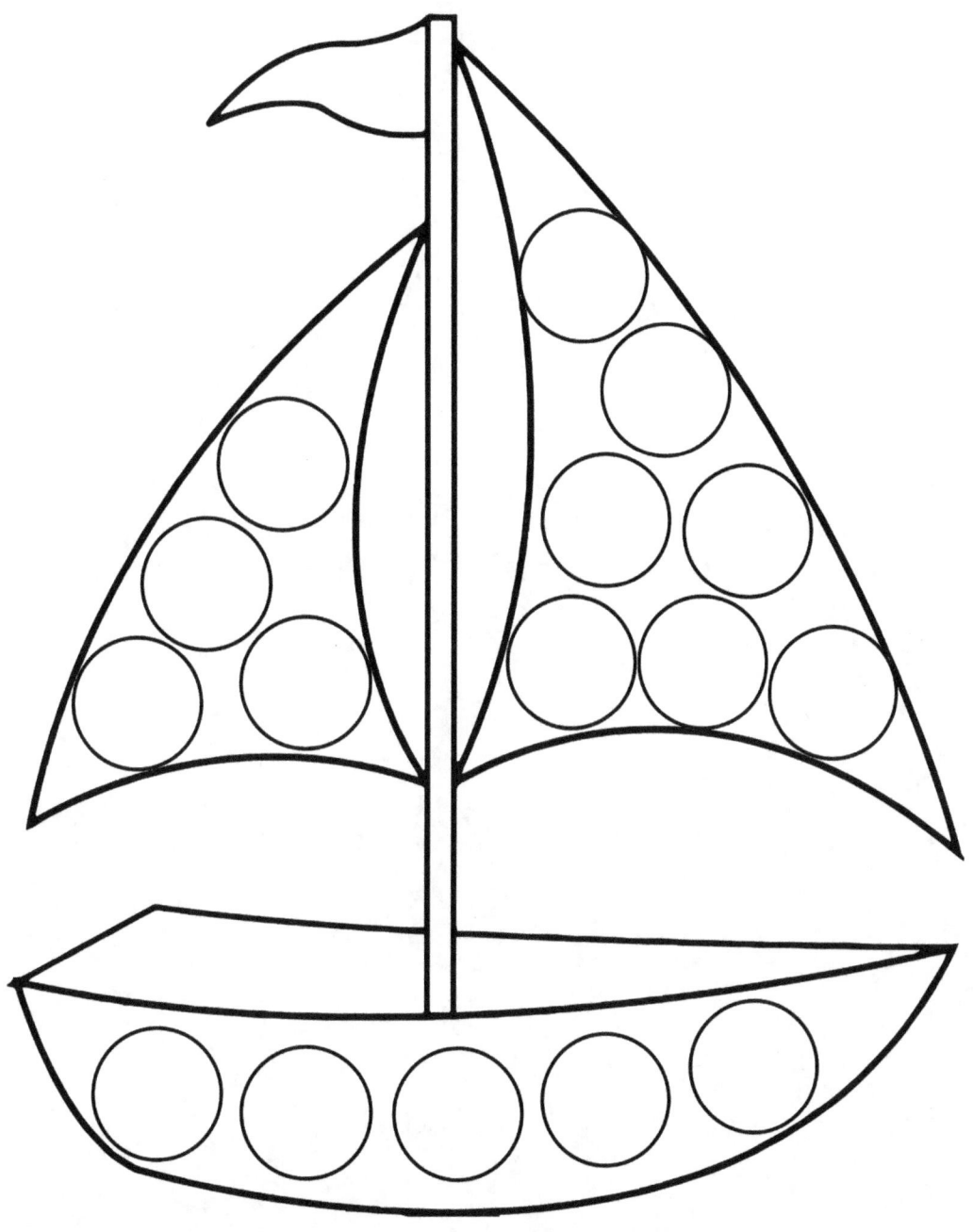

Spell out "Sailboat" by dotting each letter

S   a   i   l   b   o   a   t

Week 11

Scissor Practice

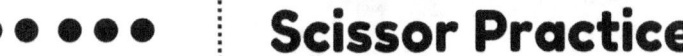

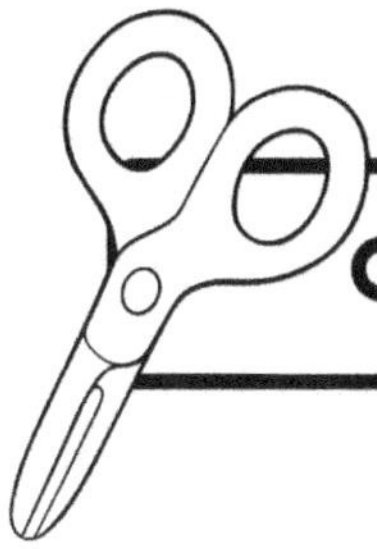

Cut along the dotted line to practice your scissor skills.

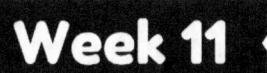

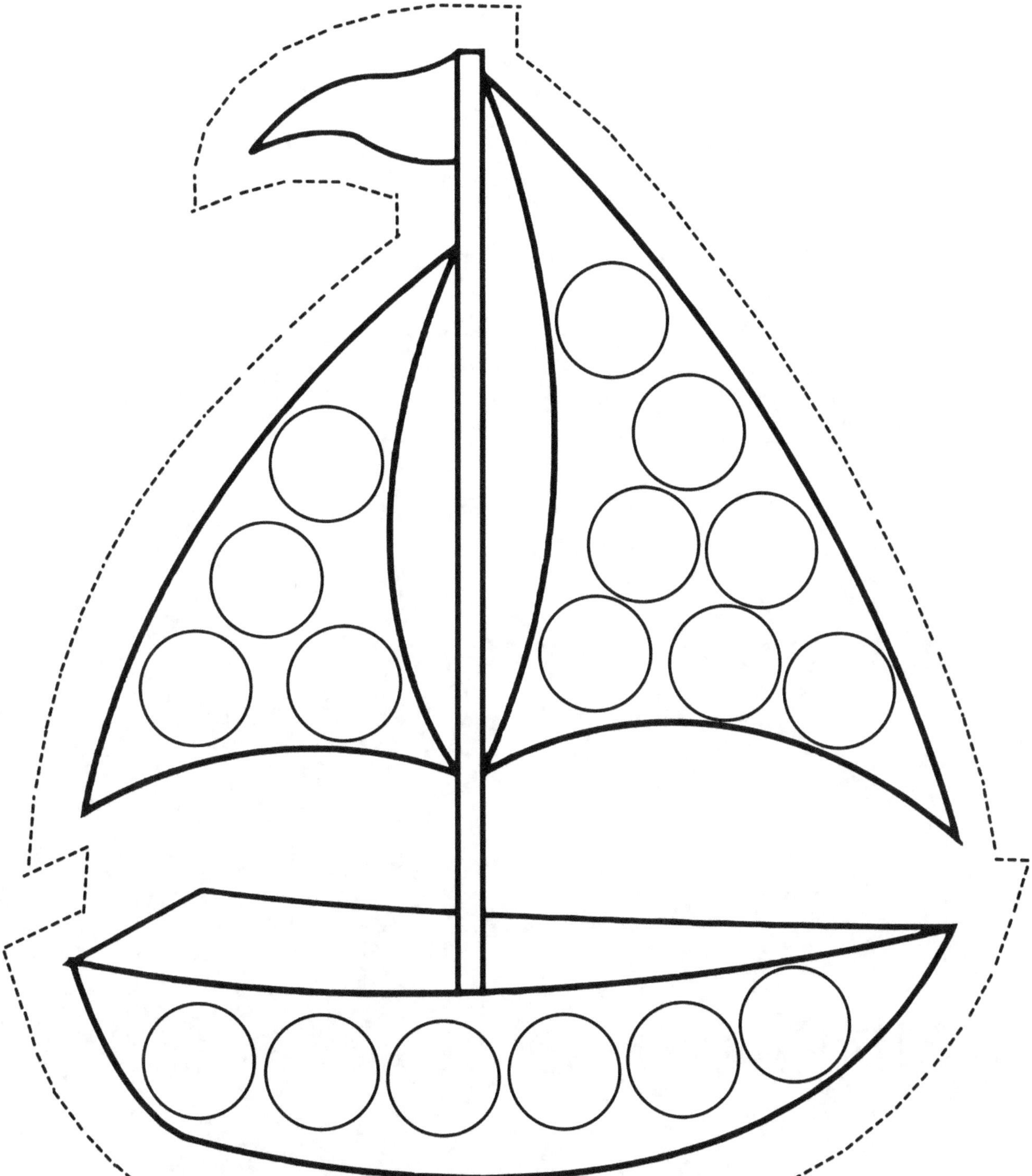

 **Find the Sailboat and dot it.**

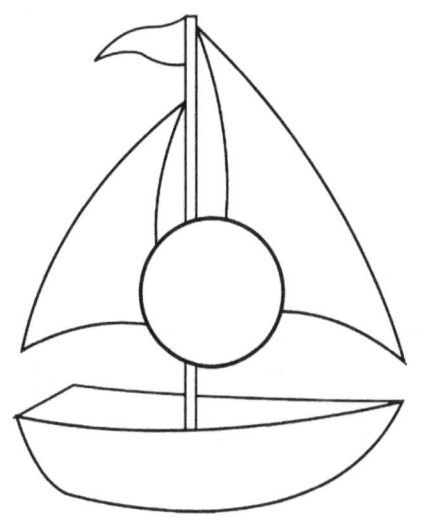

Maze

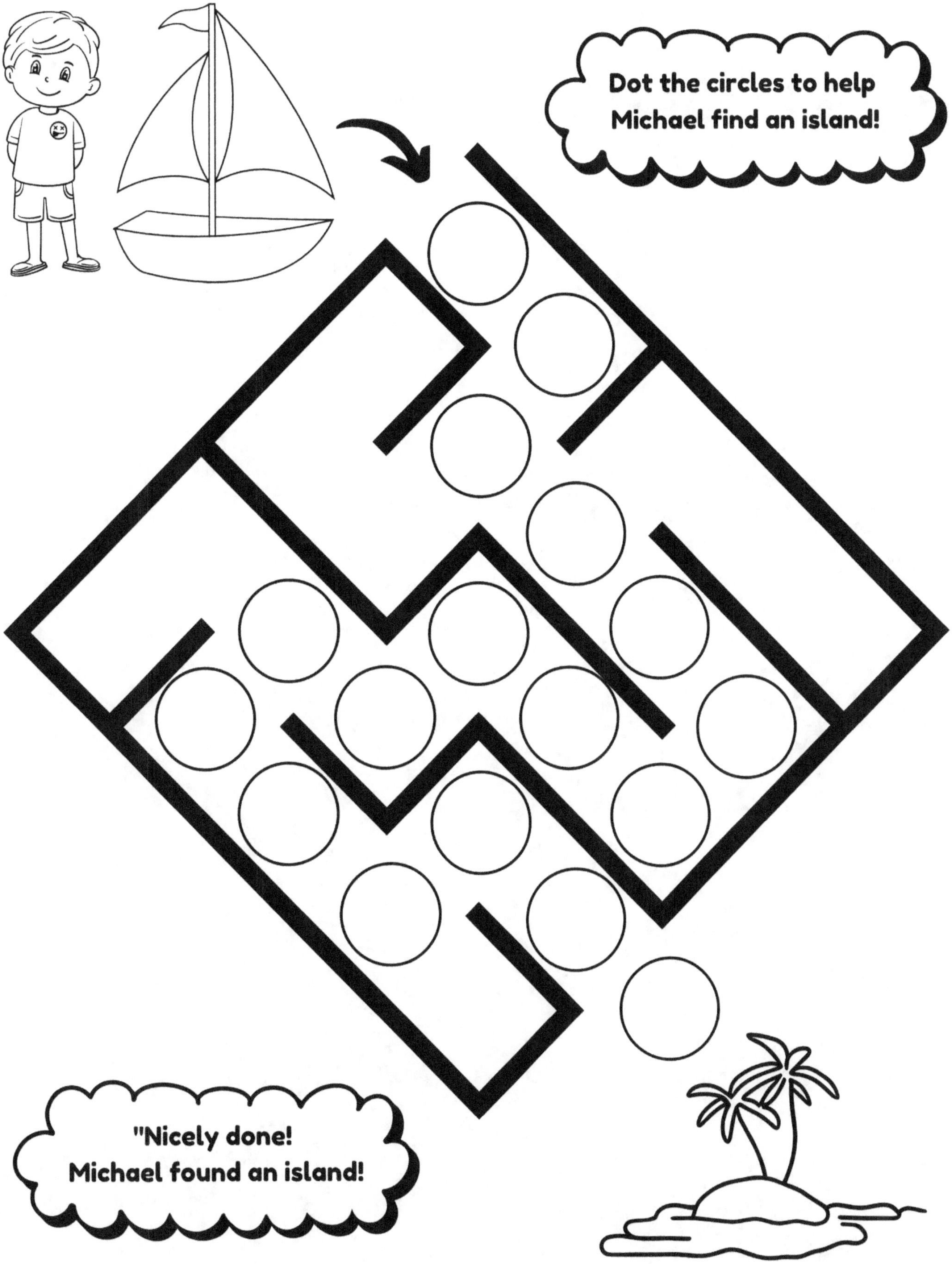

Dot the circles to help Michael find an island!

"Nicely done! Michael found an island!

Tank

Spell out "Tank" by dotting each letter

(T)   (a)   (n)   (k)

Week 12

Scissor Practice

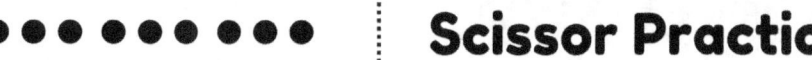

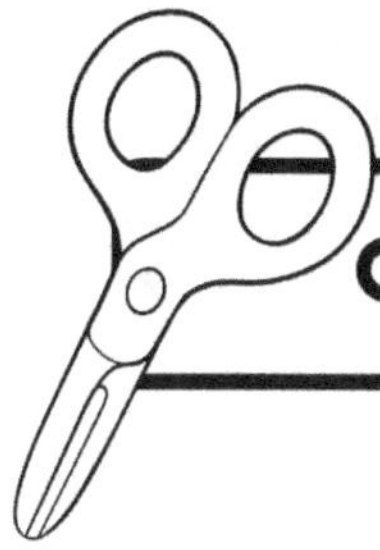

Cut along the dotted line to practice your scissor skills.

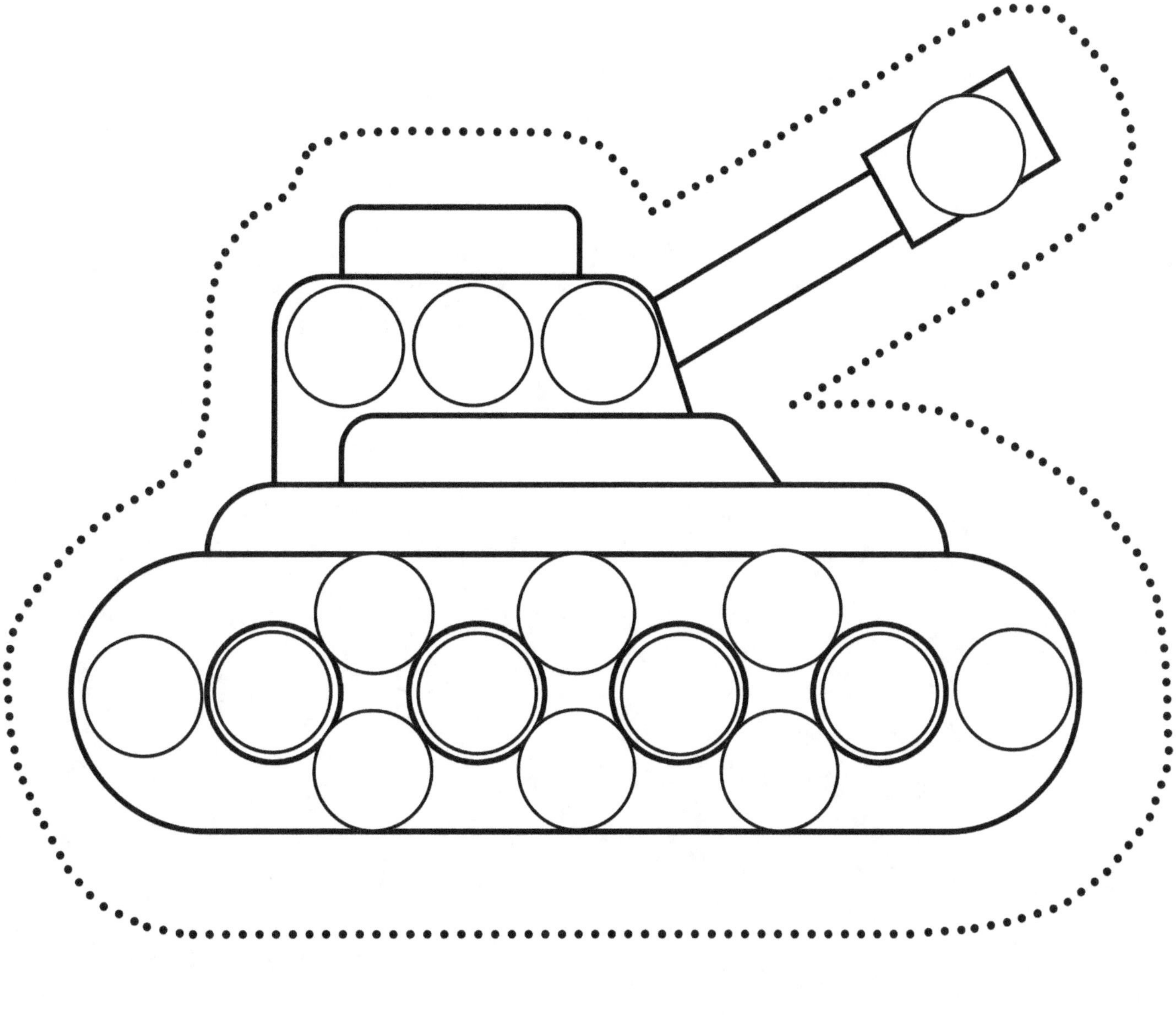

Color Match

Dot all Tanks Red

Dot all Sailboats Green

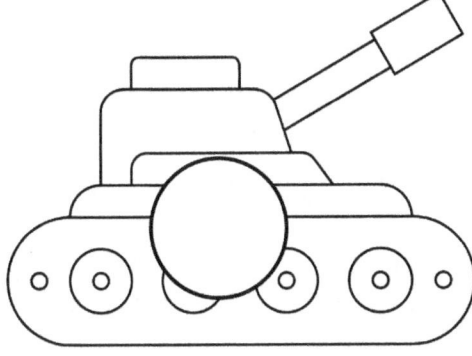
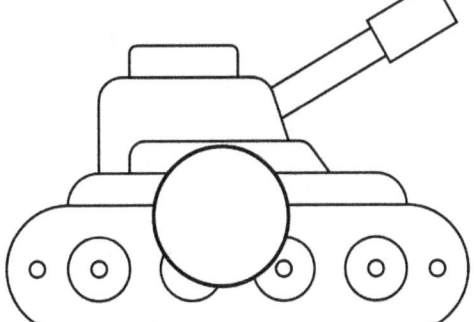
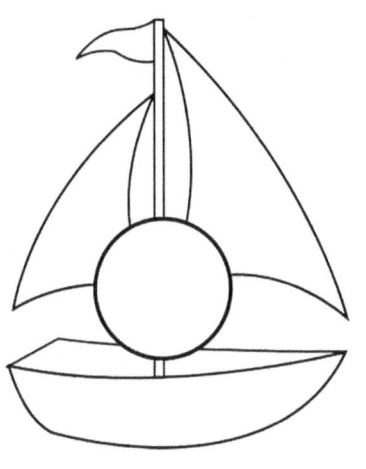
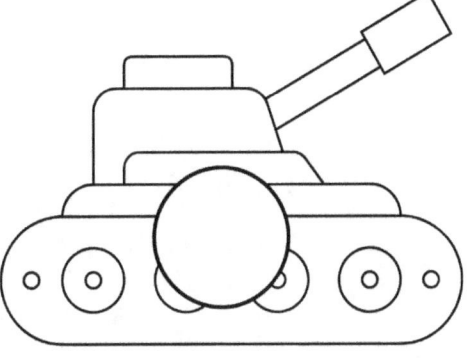
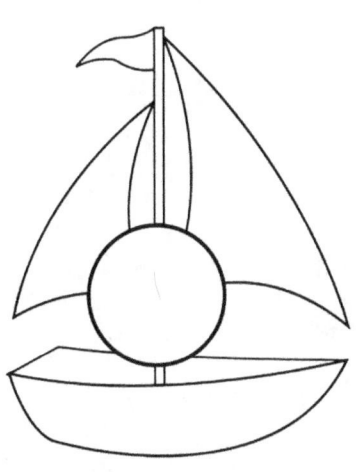

Counting

Dot 2 Tanks.

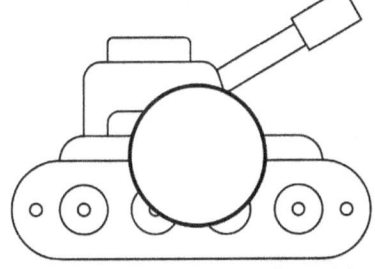

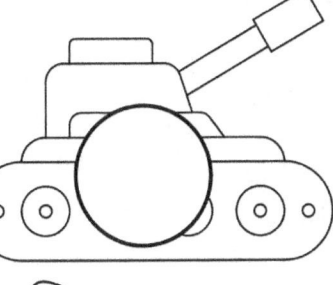
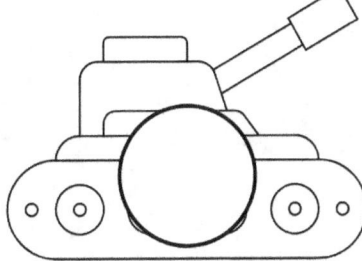
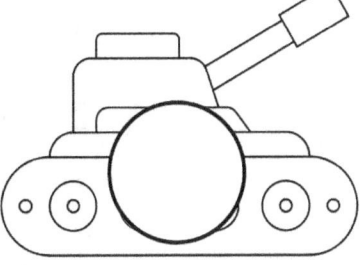

Dot 4 Sailboats.

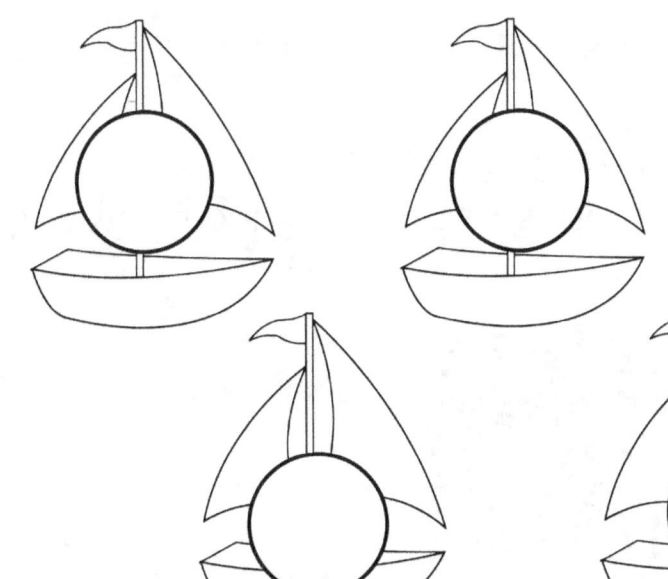
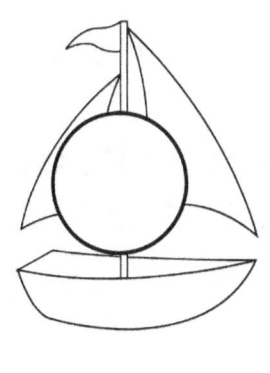
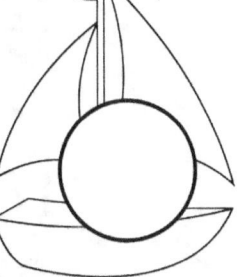

Free Printable Activity Book!

- **Enhances Creativity:** Fun dot marker coloring pages.
- **Builds Fine Motor Skills:** Scissor skill exercises and dot-to-dot puzzles.
- **Boosts Cognitive Development:** Simple addition with numbers and images.
- **Encourages Observation:** Engaging I Spy games.
- **Hours of Fun:** Full kawaii coloring pages designed for young children.

SCAN ME

Parents & Teachers!

Our biggest joy comes from helping little ones flourish and discover the world around them through learning.

That's why your thoughts matter so much to us!

Your honest thoughts about our book, even a quick sentence or two, would mean the world. We really mean it!

You'd be making a big difference for a small education brand like ours, run with love by a mother-daughter team.

Your reviews help us reach more curious minds across the globe, paving their way to success in their educational journey.

And hey, maybe we'll even sell a few more books in the process!

Every single review makes our hearts swell with gratitude.

Ready to make our day?

Scan the QR Code below to share your thoughts.